RAND EDUCATION AND LABOR

Preparing School Leaders for Success

Evaluation of New Leaders' Aspiring Principals Program, 2012–2017

Susan M. Gates, Matthew D. Baird, Christopher Joseph Doss,
Laura S. Hamilton, Isaac M. Opper, Benjamin K. Master,
Andrea Prado Tuma, Mirka Vuollo, Melanie A. Zaber

Sponsored by New Leaders

For more information on this publication, visit www.rand.org/t/RR2812

Library of Congress Cataloging-in-Publication Data is available for this publication.
ISBN: 978-1-9774-0214-1

Published by the RAND Corporation, Santa Monica, Calif.
© Copyright 2019 RAND Corporation
RAND® is a registered trademark.

Cover: GettyImages: DigitalVision/Jose Luis Pelaez Inc.

Support RAND
Make a tax-deductible charitable contribution at
www.rand.org/giving/contribute

www.rand.org

Preface

The mission of New Leaders is "to ensure high academic achievement for all children, especially students in poverty and students of color, by developing transformational school leaders and advancing the policies and practices that allow great leaders to succeed" (New Leaders, undated-b). In 2014, the RAND Corporation published an evaluation of New Leaders' Aspiring Principals program based on the outcomes of approximately 400 New Leaders principals; these principals completed the program between 2002 and 2011 and were hired as principals in school year 2011–2012 or earlier in ten current or former partner districts (Gates et al., 2014a). A follow-on effort evaluated New Leaders' Aspiring Principals program as experienced by program graduates hired as principals in the 2013–2014, 2014–2015, 2015–2016, and 2016–2017 school years in partner districts. This follow-on work was funded through a five-year U.S. Department of Education Investing in Innovation (i3) Validation Grant to New Leaders, which began in 2013 and ended in 2019.

This report presents findings from the second evaluation. We describe New Leaders' Aspiring Principals program and provide background information about New Leaders partner districts, present evidence of the program's effect on student achievement, and provide conclusions and implications based on those findings. The findings will be of interest to policymakers in school districts, charter management organizations, state education agencies, and principal-preparation programs who want to understand the effectiveness of New Leaders' Aspiring Principals program or programs with similar features. The report will also be relevant to those interested in developing approaches for assessing the effectiveness of principal-preparation programs.

This study was undertaken by RAND Education and Labor, a division of the RAND Corporation that conducts research on early childhood through postsecondary education programs, workforce development, and programs and policies affecting workers, entrepreneurship, financial literacy, and decisionmaking. This study was sponsored by New Leaders. For more information about the organization, please visit www.newleaders.org.

More information about RAND can be found at www.rand. org. Questions about this report should be directed to susan_gates@ rand.org, and questions about RAND Education and Labor should be directed to educationandlabor@rand.org.

Contents

Figures and Tables

Figures

Tables

Summary

A growing body of research points to the critical role of school leadership in student success (Herman et al., 2017). Principals build a vision and a school culture that promote equity and support student learning. They ensure that resources are used efficiently and effectively. They engage with the community. They also help promote high-quality instruction in every classroom, by hiring, monitoring, evaluating, and supporting teachers. A good principal hires the most-effective new teachers, establishes high expectations for those teachers, and provides them with feedback and support so they can continue to improve. One principal typically supervises dozens of teachers, who in turn reach hundreds or thousands of students. In spite of evidence about the ways in which principals influence classrooms and, ultimately, student achievement, calls to direct resources away from school administration and toward teachers continue (Tobias and Shorman, 2018). Meanwhile, districts across the country struggle with high levels of principal turnover (Miller, 2013; Goldring and Taie, 2014) and bear the burden of the high cost associated with principal training and onboarding—which, by some estimates, can reach $75,000 per vacancy (School Leaders Network, 2014).

The mission of New Leaders, created in 2000, is "to ensure high academic achievement for all children, especially students in poverty and students of color, by developing transformational school leaders and advancing the policies and practices that allow great leaders to succeed" (New Leaders, undated-b). The Aspiring Principals program is New Leaders' signature program and has three core features:

(1) selective recruitment and admission, (2) training and endorsement, and (3) support for principals early in their tenure (Gates et al., 2014a).

The RAND Corporation's first evaluation of the Aspiring Principals program, published in 2014, assessed the outcomes of approximately 400 New Leaders principals who completed the Aspiring Principals program between 2002 and 2011 and had been placed as principals prior to school year (SY) 2012–2013 in ten current or former partner districts (Gates et al., 2014a, 2014b). That evaluation found evidence that students who attended a school led by a New Leaders principal for three or more years experienced larger achievement gains than similar students in the same district in schools not led by a New Leaders principal.

New Leaders made major changes to core features of the Aspiring Principals program in 2012 by creating a new pathway for admission into the program, revising the residency experience to be more structured and goal-oriented, and restructuring principal induction support through a professional-learning-community approach. Aspiring principals who entered the program in SY 2012–2013, as part of Cohort 12, were the first to experience these major revisions.

Study Purpose and Approach

This report is a follow-up to our 2014 evaluation of New Leaders' Aspiring Principals program (Gates et al., 2014a). Focusing on the revised program, which was implemented starting in SY 2012–2013, this report presents evidence of the effectiveness of the revised Aspiring Principals program and shares lessons that can inform principal-preparation policy and practice.

The primary objective of the study was to understand the relationship of New Leaders' Aspiring Principals program to school and student outcomes. Our analyses assessed whether schools and students led by these New Leaders principals outperformed comparison schools and students. Therefore, the evaluation compared New Leaders principals with other new principals in the same district with respect to (1) achievement and other outcomes of the schools and students and

(2) retention rates. The evaluation also examined placement rates of those who completed New Leaders' Aspiring Principals program, as well as participants' and districts' satisfaction with the Aspiring Principals program.

Our evaluation analyzed the outcomes of schools and students in the following districts, which all had an active partnership with New Leaders during the study: Baltimore City Public Schools in Maryland, Charlotte-Mecklenburg Schools in North Carolina, Chicago Public Schools in Illinois, District of Columbia Public Schools, the New York City Department of Education, Oakland Unified School District in California, Prince George's County Public Schools in Maryland, and Shelby County Schools in Tennessee. The evaluation also included schools and students overseen by the DC Public Charter School Board.

Because research suggests that it takes time for a principal to affect achievement outcomes, we report on outcomes observed at least three years after a principal has been placed; thus, our study scope was limited to New Leaders principals who completed the Aspiring Principals program in SY 2012–2013 or later and were subsequently hired by partner districts starting in SY 2013–2014. Therefore, only schools that received a new principal in SY 2013–2014 or 2014–2015 contributed to our estimates.

When analyzing student outcomes at the school or student level, we estimated the effects by district and then averaged them across partner districts. We employed two approaches to weighting the results across districts. One approach weights the results by the number of schools studied. This "school-exposure" approach tells us the average effect of New Leaders across the entire sample of affected schools, which means districts that have more New Leaders principals will contribute more to these estimates. A second approach, which we describe as "average by district," takes a simple average of effects across partner districts. This approach tells us the average effect of the program across districts, answering the question of whether the average district might expect to benefit from the program.

Findings

Our findings highlight a number of accomplishments of the Aspiring Principals program. We refer to results as statistically significant if they were significant at the 5 percent or lower level, unless otherwise noted, meaning that there is at least a 95 percent chance that the true effect is greater than zero.

K–8 Schools Led by New Leaders Principals Outperformed K–8 Schools Led by Other New Principals in Schoolwide Student Achievement

Our analysis found a positive relationship between Aspiring Principals program principals and schoolwide student achievement in mathematics and English language arts (ELA) in K–8 schools. We found that, after three or more years, achievement in schools that received a New Leaders principal was 3.26 to 3.55 percentile points higher in mathematics and 1.81 to 2.27 percentile points higher in ELA than achievement in schools that received a new principal who was not a New Leader. In each case, percentile gains indicate how much higher an average student would be expected to perform (e.g., going from the 50th percentile in mathematics to the 53rd percentile) as a result of being in a school led by a New Leaders principal. We found larger effects using the "school exposure" approach to weighting, compared with the "average by district" approach. Both the mathematics and ELA results were statistically significant even after correcting for multiple comparisons. These results were larger than the year-three effect estimates reported in our 2014 study, where we found an effect of 1.3 percentile points in mathematics and 0.7 percentile points in ELA. That study used a student-level approach similar to the one described below.

Because so few New Leaders principals were placed immediately into high schools, we were unable to examine high school outcomes in this analysis of schoolwide effects.

Individual-Level Academic Performance and Student Attendance Were Higher for Students Who Attended K–8 Schools with a New Leaders Principal

When looking at the effect of principals who had participated in the Aspiring Principals program on student-level achievement, we analyzed the outcomes for individual students in K–8 schools and high schools who spent time both in schools led by New Leaders principals and in schools not led by New Leaders principals. We found a positive and statistically significant effect for K–8 students exposed to a New Leaders principal for three or more years, compared with K–8 students in the same district exposed to a new principal from other training programs. These effects were positive and large (around 3 to 5 percentile points) and statistically significant for ELA and mathematics using the "average by district" weighting approach. As with the school-level results, these results were more than twice as large as those reported in our 2014 study, which used a similar methodology. When we used the "school exposure" weighting approach to pool the estimates, the relationships between K–8 student outcomes and New Leaders principals were not statistically significant.

Examining attendance outcomes for K–8 students, we found a statistically significant and positive effect for principals in their third and later years in the same school. Attendance rates at elementary and middle schools averaged between 0.1 and 0.7 percentage points higher using the "average by district" weighting approach, which corresponds to between one-fifth of a school day and 1.26 more school days attended.

At the high school level, most of our results were not significant, suggesting either that too few New Leaders principals were immediately placed into high schools to detect an effect or that having a New Leaders principal does not affect student-level achievement at the high school level.

New Principals Who Completed the Aspiring Principals Program Were More Likely Than Other New Principals in the Same Districts to Remain at Their Schools as Principals for a Second Year

The average two-year retention rate for principals who participated in the Aspiring Principals program was higher than that of other newly hired principals in the same districts; however, we found no statistically significant difference between the likelihood of New Leaders principals and other principals to remain a third year.

New Leaders Principals Displayed Competencies in the Aspiring Principals Program Related to School, Student, and Principal Retention Outcomes

At the time of this report, New Leaders assessed the competencies of aspiring principals on five broad standards: (1) Personal Leadership, (2) Instructional Leadership, (3) Cultural Leadership, (4) Adult and Team Leadership, and (5) Operational Leadership. We examined the relationship between each standard and student outcomes. We also grouped competencies into three constructs using exploratory factor analysis: Human Capital (Instructional Leadership and Adult and Team Leadership), Cultural Capital (Cultural Leadership and Operational Leadership), and Personal Leadership.

When looking at individual standards, we found that Standards 2 (Instructional Leadership) and 4 (Adult and Team Leadership) showed the greatest association with student outcomes. A 1 standard deviation increase in Adult and Team Leadership (a 0.24-point increase on a four-point scale) was significantly related to a 0.030 standard deviation increase in average student mathematics performance (1.19 percentile points) and a 0.044 standard deviation increase in ELA performance (1.76 percentile points). A 1 standard deviation increase in Instructional Leadership (0.24 of one point on a four-point scale) was associated with marginally significant increases in mathematics performance (0.028 standard deviations or 1.10 percentile points) and ELA performance (0.025 standard deviations or 0.99 percentile points). Scores on the other standards were not significantly associated with student, school, or retention outcomes.

When looking at constructs, we found that the Human Capital construct was robustly associated with student outcomes. A 1 standard deviation increase in this factor was associated with a significant 0.035 standard deviation increase in ELA performance, a 0.045 standard deviation increase in mathematics performance, and a half of a percentage point improvement in attendance. The Cultural Capital construct was not significantly related to any student outcome, with all point estimates small and insignificant. However, it was related to higher principal retention, which is an important outcome, given the high costs associated with training and onboarding new principals (Miller, 2013; Goldring and Taie, 2014; School Leaders Network, 2014). The Personal Leadership construct was significantly related only to mathematics achievement. A 1 standard deviation increase in the construct was associated with a 0.016 standard deviation decrease in mathematics achievement.

A Large Share of Aspiring Principals Program Completers Were Hired into Principal Positions by Partner Districts

Between 26.2 percent and 39.3 percent of Aspiring Principals program graduates were hired as a principal by a partner district immediately after program completion. Taking a longer view, two-thirds of SY 2012–2013 graduates were placed within five years of completing the program. These placement rates are substantially higher than rates reported in a recent study of several principal-preparation programs in Tennessee. Specifically, Grissom, Mitani, and Woo (2018) found that, across ten principal-preparation programs in that state, five-year placement rates (measured from the time principals took the licensure exam) varied between 6 percent and 17 percent.

Aspiring Principals Program Participants and Partner Districts Viewed the Program Favorably

The Aspiring Principals program residents surveyed in 2016 on a nationally normed survey rated the program highly, with average ratings that were equivalent to or higher than ratings by participants of other principal-preparation programs nationwide. In particular, the Aspiring Principals program ratings were higher than those in a national sample of individuals enrolled in principal-preparation programs in the areas of Instructional Leadership, Peer Relationships, and Internship Design and Quality. The Aspiring Principals program results were similarly high in other years in which the survey was conducted but for which a national sample of results is not available for comparison.

Overall, leaders in partner districts reported that partnership with New Leaders has benefited their districts and that New Leaders principals who had been placed in those districts in the last few years were well prepared and of high quality. For example, on a five-point rating scale from 1 to 5, the district leaders we interviewed in 2017 rated their perception of the overall benefits of the New Leaders program to the district at 3.8, on average. The same year, out of all the statements posed in the study to district leaders, the statement "New Leaders is responsive to issues or concerns raised by our district/CMO [charter management organization]" received the highest level of agreement, with a rating of 4.2; the statement "New Leaders has influenced how our district/CMO selects new principals" received the lowest level of agreement, with an average rating of 2.4.

Study Limitations

The preparation, hiring, support, and retention of effective new principals is a complex, multistaged process that does not easily lend itself to a traditional experimental study design. To evaluate the effect of New Leaders principals, we relied on quasi-experimental methods. Therefore, evidence of causal effects should be interpreted with caution. Since aspiring principals were not randomly assigned to schools and students, it is possible that New Leaders and non–New Leaders principals were placed in schools that differed systematically in ways that we as evaluators could not observe, and thus could not account for. Such nonrandom sorting of principals to schools and students could have biased our estimates either positively or negatively. Moreover, since our analysis compared New Leaders principals with their peer novice principals in the same districts, our results are partially influenced by the districts' broader hiring, placement, and new-principal support efforts.

The findings in this study may be of interest to officials in large urban districts or CMOs that resemble New Leaders partner districts, who may be interested in developing or supporting programs that train and support principals. This study was focused on the unique context of the large, urban districts that partnered with New Leaders during the time frame covered by this study. Although this may limit the generalizability of our findings, the findings may be relevant for other types of districts as well. Our findings may also be of interest to researchers studying principal-preparation programs and to principal-preparation program directors and faculty who seek to understand the relationships between participants' competencies and longer-term outcomes.

Finally, our evaluation examined outcomes of graduates of a preparation program with three core features, as described above. We were not able to modify implementation of the program to test whether one or more of the core features of the Aspiring Principals program were more or less effective than others. As a result, we cannot comment on the relative value of any one feature or effective ways to modify the implementation of those features.

Conclusions and Implications

Our findings suggest the following conclusions about the value of New Leaders' Aspiring Principals program:

- New Leaders' Aspiring Principals program produced candidates who were hired at high rates and were retained on the job longer than other new principals.
- Students in K–8 schools led by principals who completed the Aspiring Principals program outperformed students in K–8 schools led by other new principals.
- Data gathered by New Leaders about participants' competencies may be helpful for predicting those same participants' performance after graduation.

We draw the following implications for policymakers, program designers, and researchers about the Aspiring Principals program and about principal-preparation programs more generally.

Evaluations of Principal-Preparation Programs Should Examine Multiple Program Features and Outcomes

Evaluations of principal-preparation programs face special challenges because of small sample sizes, the infeasibility of experimental design, and difficulty in distinguishing the effects of preparation programs from other experiences that principals have after attending such programs. By looking at a range of outcomes at the principal, school, and student levels, our evaluation provides a rich characterization of the ways in which principal-preparation programs influence districts and their schools and students.

Principal-Preparation Programs Can Help Build Internal Capacity Within Partner Districts

Through a long-term partnership approach, principal-preparation programs like New Leaders can influence more than just the quality of principal candidates. Several of the district officials we have interviewed over the years described New Leaders as a thought partner and said that New Leaders had influenced overall district leadership standards, hiring, and evaluation.

Within- and Between-District Analyses Could Provide Complementary Evidence Regarding Program Effectiveness

Many evaluations of principal-preparation programs rely on within-district comparisons. However, districts that are effective at hiring, placing, and supporting new principals likely experience less variation in the quality of newly placed principals. In turn, this makes it more difficult to use within-district comparisons to identify differences among principals from varying pre-service programs. Between-district analysis would allow for a comparison against principals hired by other districts that might not have such robust hiring practices or other supports in place. Comparing school outcomes for new principals in other districts would be a useful approach to understanding the systemic effects of partnering with an organization such as New Leaders, providing evidence that complements the findings from a within-district analysis.

Multiyear Evaluations Are Needed to Capture the Effect of Program Features on School Outcomes

For a principal-preparation program such as New Leaders to affect students, participants must complete the program, be hired as principals, and remain in their positions long enough to have an effect on schools and students. This process can take many years. As a result, it is crucial to take a long-term perspective, supporting program evaluation and tracking outcomes over many years.

Acknowledgments

We would like to thank the United States Department of Education for supporting this work through an Investing in Innovation (i3) grant. We would like to thank the many employees of school districts, charter management organizations, and states who participated in interviews, considered our data requests, provided us with data, and fielded our questions over the years. We are especially grateful to the district officials who provided feedback on our district profiles. We would also like to thank a number of current and former RAND colleagues who made important contributions to this work: Diana C. Lavery, Mark A. Harris, Alyssa Ramos, Emilio Chavez-Herrerias, Juliana Chen-Peraza, Amanda Edelman, Crystal Huang, Ashley Muchow, Claudia Rodriguez, and Joshua Russell-Fritch helped with data cleaning and analysis. Susan Burkhauser and Crystal Huang assisted with interviews and qualitative data gathering. Numerous RAND colleagues provided feedback on this research during seminars. We are especially grateful to Fatih Unlu and Cathy Stasz for their detailed comments on our interim reports and on an earlier draft of this document. Paco Martorell contributed to the project design. We are grateful to Jason Grissom of Vanderbilt University and Cathy Stasz of RAND for reviewing an earlier draft of this report. Rebecca Fowler carefully edited the final copy, and Monette Velasco effectively managed the production of the final report.

We are grateful to Marcy Reedy, of the University Council for Educational Administration, for helping us to access data from the INSPIRE survey responses from Aspiring Principals program participants. We are indebted to Barbara Goodsen and Cris Price of ABT

Associates. As technical support providers for this i3 grant, they provided expert guidance on how to understand the changing What Works Clearinghouse standards and how to apply them effectively to our evaluation design. They also provided feedback on the technical sections of an earlier draft of this report.

We are grateful to current and former contacts at New Leaders, who provided us with data and input that were critical to this research. Brenda Neuman-Sheldon, Marianna Valdez, Gina Ikemoto, Jackie Gran, Jean Desravines, Ben Fenton, Rayanne Mroczek, and other staff at New Leaders provided invaluable input on this research, including feedback on interim reports and on an earlier draft of this report.

Abbreviations

CMO	charter management organization
DCPS	District of Columbia Public Schools
ELA	English language arts
ELL	English language learner
SY	school year
UCEA	University Council for Educational Administration
WWC	What Works Clearinghouse

CHAPTER ONE

Introduction

A growing body of research points to the critical role of school leadership in student success (Herman et al., 2017). Principals build a vision and a school culture that promote equity and support student learning. They ensure that resources are used efficiently and effectively. They engage with the community. They also help promote high-quality instruction in every classroom, by hiring, monitoring, evaluating, and supporting teachers. A good principal hires the most-effective new teachers, establishes high expectations for those teachers, and provides them with feedback and support so they can continue to improve. One principal typically supervises dozens of teachers, who in turn reach hundreds or thousands of students. In spite of evidence about the ways in which principals influence classrooms and, ultimately, student achievement, calls to direct resources away from school administration and toward teachers continue (Tobias and Shorman, 2018).

The mission of New Leaders, created in 2000, is "to ensure high academic achievement for all children, especially students in poverty and students of color, by developing transformational school leaders and advancing the policies and practices that allow great leaders to succeed" (New Leaders, undated-b). New Leaders partners with districts and charter management organizations (CMOs) to offer rigorous, research-based training for aspiring principals and to improve the conditions in which those school leaders work (Gates et al., 2014a). In school year (SY) 2001–2002, the first cohort of aspiring principals completed a structured residency-based program as part of New Leaders' Aspiring Principals program in New York City and Chicago. The Aspiring Principals program would become New Leaders' signature program as it expanded its partnerships across the nation and developed new program offerings. New Leaders has refined the Aspiring Principals program in response to the needs of districts and program participants and in response to its evaluation findings. Even with these refinements, three core features of the Aspiring Principals program have endured since 2001: (1) selective recruitment and admissions, (2) training and endorsement, and (3) support for principals early in their tenure (Gates et al., 2014a, p. xvi).

In 2006, New Leaders contracted with the RAND Corporation to conduct a formative and summative evaluation of the program, of its theory of action, and of its implementation. In 2014, we published a report using data on the outcomes of approximately 400 New Leaders principals who had completed the Aspiring Principals program between 2002 and 2011 and were placed as principals prior to SY 2012–2013 in ten current or former partner districts: Baltimore City Public Schools in Maryland, Charlotte-Mecklenburg Schools in North Carolina, Chicago Public Schools in Illinois, Memphis City Schools in Tennessee, Milwaukee Public Schools in Wisconsin, New Orleans Recovery School District, New York City Public Schools, Oakland Unified School District in California, Prince George's County Public Schools in Maryland, and District of Columbia Public Schools (DCPS) and the DC Public Charter School Board (Gates et al., 2014a, 2014b). That evaluation found evidence that, after three years, students in schools led by New Leaders principals experienced higher achievement gains, on average, than students in similar schools in the same districts led by non–New Leaders principals. The estimated gains were 3 percentile points for high school reading, 1.7 percentile points for lower-grade reading, and 0.7 percentile points in lower-grade mathematics achievement. The study also found evidence that these effects on achievement differed by district but could not attribute this variation to any one factor.

New Leaders made major changes to the Aspiring Principals program in 2012, by creating a new pathway for admission into the program, revising the residency experience to be more structured and goal-oriented, and restructuring induction support through a professional learning-community approach. These changes are described in more detail in Chapter Two. Aspiring principals who entered the program in SY 2012–2013, as part of Cohort 12, were the first to experience these major revisions. In 2013, New Leaders was awarded an Investing in Innovation (i3) Validation Grant from the U.S. Department of Education, which it used to contract with RAND to evaluate the outcomes of New Leaders principals trained after the program was revised.

Our evaluation analyzed the outcomes of schools and students in schools in the following districts, which had an active partnership with New Leaders during this study: Baltimore City Public Schools in Maryland, Charlotte-Mecklenburg Schools in North Carolina, Chicago Public Schools in Illinois, DCPS, the New York City Department of Education, Oakland Unified School District in California, Prince George's County Public Schools in Maryland, and Shelby County Schools in Tennessee. It also includes schools overseen by the DC Public Charter School Board.

Below, we outline our evaluation approach.

Purpose of the Report

This report is a follow-up to our 2014 evaluation of New Leaders' Aspiring Principals program (Gates et al., 2014a). It focused on the Aspiring Principals program as revised and implemented starting in the 2012–2013 school year. As shown in Figure 1.1, our 2014 report examined outcomes for individuals who completed their Aspiring Principals program residencies prior to SY 2011–2012. In this report, we studied the individuals who completed their Aspiring Principals program residencies in SY 2012–2013 through SY 2016–2017. The overarching objective of this report was to present evidence of the effectiveness of the revised Aspiring Principals program and to share lessons that could inform principal-preparation policy and practice nationwide. We aimed to understand the relationship between New Leaders' Aspiring Principals program and school and student outcomes. Our core analyses assessed whether schools (and students) led by these New Leaders

Figure 1.1
Timeline of New Leaders Cohorts, Partnerships, and Program Revisions

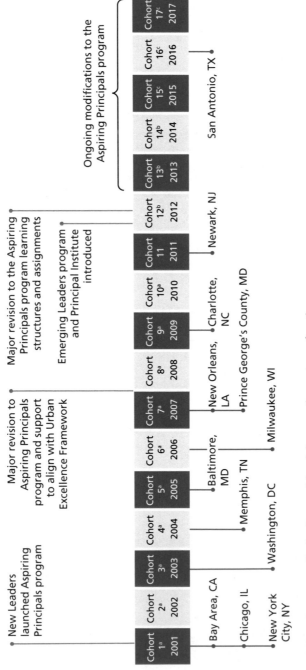

NOTE: In Tennessee, Shelby County Schools became the partner after the merger.
[a] Denotes cohorts included in prior analysis (Gates et al., 2014a).
[b] Denotes cohorts included in the analysis of program data and effects.
[c] Denotes cohorts included in the analysis of program data only.

principals outperformed comparison schools and students. To more fully understand those relationships, we also looked at information gathered during the Aspiring Principals program about the characteristics of the candidates, their competencies at different points in the program, and their placement outcomes to determine how these competencies were related to outcomes. The following six research questions structured our evaluation of the revised program.

Research Questions

1. How do the outcomes of schools and students led by New Leaders principals compare with those of other schools and students in the district?
2. Are Aspiring Principals program graduates who are hired as principals in partner districts more or less likely to stay in their position than other new-principal hires?
3. To what extent are Aspiring Principals program graduates being hired as principals in partner districts and in what types of schools?
4. What are the characteristics of the Aspiring Principals program participants?
5. To what extent are the competencies that the Aspiring Principals program participants demonstrate while they are in the program associated with placement as a principal, retention, and school or student outcomes?
6. How do Aspiring Principals program participants and partner districts view New Leaders and the Aspiring Principals program?

We addressed these questions by analyzing descriptive and statistical evidence that compared New Leaders principals with other new principals in the same districts. We examined differences in the following key outcomes:

- achievement outcomes for students of New Leaders principals (in English language arts [ELA] and mathematics)
- other outcomes for students of New Leaders principals (e.g., attendance)
- retention of New Leaders as principals in their schools.

We also analyzed data collected by New Leaders about program participants (e.g., assessments of participants' skills upon entry and completion of the program, such interim outcomes as placement) and explored whether these program data were useful indicators of future performance.

Organization of the Report

In the next chapter, we provide background information about New Leaders and the Aspiring Principals program, including a discussion of recent changes to the program. We also summarize the conditions of districts that partnered with New Leaders in the Aspiring Principals program. Chapter Three presents the data and methods we used to address the research questions, and Chapter Four provides brief summaries of key findings related to each research question. We discuss implications for the field in Chapter Five. Finally, a series of appendixes provides detailed information about the methods used and the results of each set of analyses. These appendixes are available for download at www.rand.org/t/RR2812.

CHAPTER TWO

Background

New Leaders' Aspiring Principals program operates on an annual cycle. Participants engage in a set of training experiences with other aspiring principals from the same cohort—those who were selected and began the program in the same school year. During that initial school year—also known as the residency year—candidates experience academic coursework, a yearlong residency under a mentor principal in one of the partner districts, and assessments of leadership growth. The program is provided without a fee to the aspiring principals, who work as employees of the participating school district and receive salaries during their residency years. New Leaders structured the program so that aspiring principals would not need to make excessive financial sacrifices; the aim of such a structure was to broaden the pool of potential candidates.

In this chapter,[1] we summarize the key features of effective principal-preparation programs and show how the Aspiring Principals program incorporates them; we describe the changes made to the Aspiring Principals program as of SY 2012–2013; and we give a summary of the characteristics of the New Leaders partner districts as they relate to the selection and management of principals.[2]

---

[1] Some of the material in this chapter is adapted from Gates et al., 2014a. See that report for more information about New Leaders and Aspiring Principals program features.

[2] Although the D.C. charter partners do not compose a school district, for simplicity, we use the term *district* throughout the report.

Key Features of Effective Principal-Preparation Programs

Traditional principal-preparation programs typically aim to prepare current and aspiring educators to become principals through training that combines classroom instruction and some type of school-based internship. These programs usually lead to an advanced degree or certification. Over a decade ago, a research study by Darling-Hammond et al. (2007) identified features of effective principal-preparation programs and established a basis from which experts and stakeholders developed a characterization of effective programs. This characterization encompasses program content, structure, and delivery. It also touches upon process issues, notably the importance of district partnership, the alignment of program content to standards for principals' performance on the job, and the use of data for continuous quality improvement (Darling-Hammond et al., 2007; Larsen et al., 2016a, 2016b). In this section, we define some of these key features and describe how the Aspiring Principals program incorporates them.

Strong Program-District Partnership

First, effective principal-preparation programs collaborate with school districts to ensure coherence between recruitment, training, and practice; create field experiences or internships for program participants; provide feedback on graduate quality; and/or review the curriculum and its alignment to district standards and needs. As described by Gates et al. (2014a), creating strong partnerships with districts on a selective basis has been an essential component of the Aspiring Principals program. In selecting partners, New Leaders has focused on districts that view principals as instrumental to improving the achievement of high-needs students and that are committed to providing principals with sufficient autonomy to promote change in the school. Over the years, New Leaders has used different approaches to manage district relationships, but it has always had at least one representative engage with district officials on recruitment, residency placements, and district-specific training needs. New Leaders also tracks the placement of program graduates and requests feedback from the districts regarding how graduates are performing.

Selective Recruitment and Admissions

The second key feature of effective principal-preparation programs is the rigorous recruitment of high-potential candidates who have experience as dynamic expert teachers and a commitment to instructional improvement. Selectivity in recruitment and admissions has been a core element of the Aspiring Principals program since its inception. Up until 2012, when another admission option was added (as described below), all applicants were admitted through a national recruitment and admissions process that typically involved eligibility screening and a set of admission activities designed to assess the candidate's interest in and suitability for school leadership. These activities included online exercises in which applicants demonstrated their potential in such key areas and competencies as pedagogy, communication and interpersonal relationships, standards-based planning, leadership development, data-driven decisionmaking, and urgency and efficacy (New Leaders, 2017). Those who passed the screening and online admission activities participated in a Finalist Selection Day. The Finalist Selection Day consisted of a set of virtual interviews with New Leaders staff involving exercises that tested the ability of candidates to respond to realistic leadership challenges in an urban school. For those who successfully completed the Finalist Selection Day, New Leaders staff could request an in-person interview, check the applicants' references, and work to place each candidate as a resident at a school.

Alignment to Research-Based Standards

Effective programs align their structure and curriculum to research-based standards. As described in a research-based book from New Leaders, *Breakthrough Principals* (Desravines, Aquino, and Fenton, 2016), starting in SY 2008–2009 with Cohort 8, the Aspiring Principals program structure and curriculum aligned to a research-based conceptual framework, the Transformational Leadership Framework, based on the Urban Excellence Framework. The framework outlines what New Leaders identified as key school practices that resulted in dramatic achievement gains, along with the actions that principals must take to put those practices into place. The Urban Excellence Framework was informed by a review of prior research, as well as by original research conducted by New Leaders, which included in-depth case studies of three high-achieving schools led by New Leaders principals, site visits to more than 100 New Leaders schools (both high-gaining and not) and non–New Leaders schools, and the expertise of New Leaders staff and principals (New Leaders, 2016). The framework was subsequently validated in an independent study examining the practices of schools that achieved positive value-added results (Hutchins, Epstein, and Sheldon, 2012).

Experiential Learning

Effective principal-preparation programs also provide participants with learning experiences that expose them to problems often faced in school leadership roles, with the intent to build practical and technical knowledge. Learning experiences are scaffolded, moving from classroom or online learning simulations to internship experiences, where participants lead all or a significant portion of a school's operations, including activities related to instructional leadership. Experiential learning is a key component of the Aspiring Principals program. The Summer Foundations course, offered at the beginning of the program, and the in-person group training (one to two sessions per month) include practice-oriented learning opportunities aligned with the Urban Excellence Framework and provide opportunity for reflection. More importantly, after the summer course, participants are placed in a yearlong residency under a mentor principal in one of New Leaders' partner districts. During the residency year, the resident is an employee of the district and serves in an official capacity—usually that of an assistant principal. Residents assume the responsibilities associated with their jobs while engaging in structured, hands-on learning opportunities with individualized feedback and coaching from a New Leaders staff member (typically, a former principal who was successful in improving student outcomes). The residency experience is designed to provide ample opportunity for role-playing, simulation, feedback, and reflection.

Data Use for Continuous Quality Improvement

Another common feature of high-quality preparation programs is the use of data for continuous quality improvement. These programs seek out evidence of whether and how their training is advancing leadership practices, school culture, or student learning. This process involves having established routines for collecting program-effectiveness information and using data to adjust the curriculum and program structure. Since its inception, New Leaders has set high, outcome-oriented standards; monitored performance against those standards; and modified the program as needed in response to the performance data. For example, in earlier years, the residency focused on building general skills, such as data-driven decisionmaking and personal leadership. Now, there is an emphasis on developing specific hands-on skills in priority areas and having residents practice using those skills. New Leaders also monitors participants' progress throughout the residency year using ongoing assessments. The assessments measure the extent to which each resident is making progress toward the desired principal competencies. New Leaders uses the results to inform program activities and support both during residency and after placement as a principal.

On-the-Job Support After Program Completion

Finally, a feature shared by many effective principal-preparation programs is intensive on-the-job support—in the form of mentoring, coaching, or peer networking for program graduates who are hired as principals for at least one year after graduation. Such New Leaders support is grounded in ongoing assessment and the needs of the school. This program element has gone through changes over time and has varied by district in intensity and structure but has been a consistent feature of the program.

Changes to New Leaders' Aspiring Principals Program Affecting Cohort 12 and Subsequent Cohorts

New Leaders made significant changes to improve the Aspiring Principals program and to provide structured support for new principals though professional learning communities. These changes were informed by interim findings from the 2014 RAND evaluation and a subsequent analysis by New Leaders to understand the factors driving evaluation results. The changes were instituted in 2011 and 2012, so they did not affect the group of principals included in our 2014 evaluation, who had already graduated from the program. Hence, this evaluation focuses on the effects of the revised Aspiring Principals program starting in SY 2012–2013 with Cohort 12. A detailed description of changes made to the Aspiring Principals program between 2001 and 2011 can be found in our 2014 report. Here, we detail the changes that New Leaders instituted in 2012 or later.

Creation of the Emerging Leaders Program
For the first 12 years of the program, entry into the Aspiring Principals program was solely through the national recruitment and admissions process. That changed in 2012 with the introduction of the Emerging Leaders program, created in response to a need to build the pool of leadership talent within the current partner districts. Research by New Leaders and RAND (Burkhauser et al., 2012) had identified adult leadership skills—the skills needed to lead a team of adults to raise student achievement—as an important but often lacking characteristic of aspiring principals. The Emerging Leaders program was designed to address this gap by providing teacher leaders and assistant principals interested in the principalship with opportunities to develop these adult leadership skills—such skills as getting teachers to buy in to proposed changes and building a sense of urgency for change. The program works by recruiting promising teachers, instructional coaches, and assistant principals in partner districts who seek to become principals and then leading them through a year of experiential learning and mentoring with a focus on building their skills in leading a team of adults to raise student achievement. Participants are assessed at the end of the program, and, according to their performance, they may be invited to enroll in the Aspiring Principals program. The creation of this program is relevant to our current evaluation because it could have affected the pool of applicants for the Aspiring Principals program starting in SY 2013–2014 (Cohort 13).

Improving the Aspiring Principals Program

Besides introducing the Emerging Leaders program, New Leaders instituted several changes to the Aspiring Principals program starting in 2012. First, each resident became responsible for identifying and working toward a set of specific, measurable, achievable, relevant, and time-bound goals and was assigned supervision of four teachers. The residents' performance was assessed, in part, by their success in helping those teachers improve student achievement. Second, New Leaders identified and incorporated 15 leadership actions into the program, which residents were expected to repeatedly practice and receive feedback on. Third, the program incorporated standard assignments that all residents completed to demonstrate proficiency in the standards assessed for endorsement. Finally, over time, the Aspiring Principals program became more hands-on, goal-oriented, and tied to the daily work of the resident in his or her school.

Ongoing Changes Since 2012

Since implementing these major programmatic changes in 2012, New Leaders has continued to modify the programs based on analysis of interim outcome data and feedback from district partners and program participants.

New Leaders also offers programs and approaches not directly linked with the Aspiring Principals program. These include a suite of training and support activities for sitting principals and their instructional leadership teams within their specific school context. In addition, beginning in 2015, New Leaders implemented its principal-supervisor support program. This program works with a district's central office, which is responsible for managing and supervising the district's principals, with the idea that the alignment of principal supervisors with New Leaders' mission and training fosters conditions for principal success.

As New Leaders has adjusted its programs and activities over time, the organization itself has also evolved to facilitate these changes. In 2015, New Leaders made significant alterations to the structure of its leadership team and its organization. First, at the local level, responsibility for programs was separated from responsibility for external relations, and clear functional reporting chains were established. Second, some city offices were combined into regions. Third, throughout the New Leaders organization, roles and responsibilities were aligned around functional expertise, with an associated change in reporting relationships.

Conditions in New Leaders Partner Districts

Conditions in the local districts and in the districts' principal pipe-line activities influence the residency experience, the number of individuals hired as principals, the schools in which they are placed, and the working conditions they experience when they become principals. In this section, we provide a brief characterization of district-context elements that affect alternative pre-service options, the availability of placements, and working conditions faced by New Leaders residents or principals. We include more-detailed information about the district context in Appendix A.

Training Principals

In the past ten years, many New Leaders partner districts have worked to develop partnerships with other principal-preparation programs and to build their own capacity to train principals. Therefore, six districts in the study had partnerships with programs other than New Leaders during the study period. For example, Chicago Public Schools works with a total of ten principal-preparation programs, all of which include residencies. Five districts developed their own district-run principal-preparation programs. The earliest was Prince George's County Public Schools, which launched its own program in 2012. Baltimore City Public Schools and DCPS adopted their own programs in 2013, the New York City Department of Education in 2014, and Shelby County in 2015. Three of these districts, having decided to build their capacity for this work in-house, eventually ended their Aspiring Principals program partnerships with New Leaders—Prince George's County Public Schools, DCPS, and the New York City Department of Education.

Principal Selection

Despite district investment in the program, New Leaders partnership does not lead to automatic placement. Rather, the graduates of the program go through the same hiring and placement process as other qualified candidates. New Leaders was one of the first programs to use a rigorous and selective process to select candidates for the Aspiring Principals program. Seven New Leaders partner districts have developed similar processes to screen applicants for the principalship into a candidate pool from which principal placements for individual schools are made. Selection into the candidate pools usually involves competency assessments and several rounds of interviews. Oakland Unified has developed a rigorous application process for open principal positions. In the New Orleans Recovery School District and among D.C. public charter schools, individual charter schools had the autonomy to institute their own selection processes.

Supporting Novice Principals

In addition to developing their own capacity to train and select principals, many New Leaders partner districts also launched support processes for new principals. Five districts provided targeted support for new principals for at least a year, in the form of mentoring, coaching, or ongoing professional-development opportunities. For example, Charlotte-Mecklenburg supported novice principals during their first five years, Chicago organized professional development for first-year principals, DCPS provided one-year mentorship for new principals, the New York City Department of Education supported new principals through one-on-one coaching, and Prince George's County provided a mentoring system for new principals.

Challenges in Evaluating the Effects of Principal-Preparation Programs

An evaluation of the link between school outcomes and a principal-preparation program is difficult because (1) it takes time for a principal to have an effect on student outcomes, (2) school and student outcomes are influenced by factors other than the characteristics of the principal, and (3) the characteristics of a new principal are influenced not only by the principal-preparation program but also by many other factors.

The relationships between the program and any of its effects are likely mediated by a number of factors, as described in Figure 2.1 and elaborated on later.

It Takes Time for a Principal to Influence School Outcomes, and Leadership Transitions Can Be Disruptive Initially

The activities through which principals influence student achievement take time to implement and bear fruit—vision-setting, hiring effective teachers, developing a positive school culture, and providing support for teachers' professional development (Rangel, 2018). Implementing such activities could be temporarily disruptive to the school, a theory that is consistent with research showing evidence of decreases in achievement outcomes among schools that get a new principal (Branch, Hanushek, and Rivkin, 2012; Béteille, Kalogrides, and Loeb, 2012; Burkhauser

Figure 2.1
Relationship Between New Leaders and School Outcomes

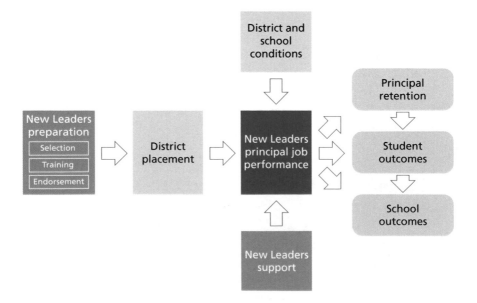

et al., 2012). Miller (2013) found that achievement in North Carolina elementary schools declined prior to a principal transition and then continued to decline for two years after the principal transition. Coelli and Green (2012) found evidence that the effect of a new principal on student outcomes grows over time. The authors estimated that by the principal's third year, the effect is approximately two-thirds of the "full effect" that might eventually be realized.

School Outcomes Are Influenced by Factors Other Than the Principal
Principal-preparation programs strive to produce graduates who will be effective school leaders. Although programs sometimes do track short-term outcomes, such as participant satisfaction, competency growth, and certification and placement rates, stakeholders are most interested in whether the schools led by candidates from a particular program have a positive effect on teacher and student outcomes (Cheney and Davis, 2011), a topic on which there is limited research (George W. Bush Institute, 2016). Research has demonstrated that effective principals raise student achievement and are an important factor in driving improved student and teacher outcomes (Leithwood et al., 2004; Branch, Hanushek, and Rivken, 2012; Coelli and Green, 2012; Grissom, Kalogrides, and Loeb, 2015).

A number of other factors, such as teacher characteristics, family backgrounds, and baseline student characteristics, have been shown to influence individual-level student outcomes. Some of these factors can be partially addressed by controlling for them in a regression analysis to the extent possible. Working conditions—such as principal autonomy, school supports provided by the district, and professional-development and mentoring opportunities—make up another set of factors that are less often considered or accounted for in analyses of the relationship between principals and school outcomes. Additionally, as we noted in our prior report (Gates et al., 2014a), evaluating the effect of preparation programs by comparing the outcomes of program principals with other principals in the same district is different from predicting the effect a graduate from a particular program will have on a school or students. Strong candidates from a particular preparation program might be more likely to outperform other new principals in a district that is ineffective in selecting new principals and offering them autonomy and support and less likely to outperform other new principals in a district that is effective in those roles.

Over Time, Practices of Partner Districts Increasingly Reflected Core Features of the Aspiring Principals Program

Over time, the ten New Leaders partner districts that participated in our study have adopted or strengthened their own principal pipeline activities in ways that resemble the Aspiring Principals program. These changes could mean that, throughout our study period, non–New Leaders principals in partner districts might have graduated from principal-preparation programs that incorporated some of the key features of the Aspiring Principals program—for example, going through rigorous selection processes similar to those of the Aspiring Principals program, receiving early on-the-job coaching and mentoring, and participating in ongoing performance assessments. In other words, improvements in districts' principal pipeline activities could have exposed some or all of their non–New Leaders principals to elements that define the Aspiring Principals program, thus dampening the contrast between principals who participated in the Aspiring Principals program and those who did not.

An analysis of program effectiveness should thus consider multiple program outcomes and clearly describe the comparison groups used to analyze different outcomes.[3]

Characteristics of a New Principal Are Influenced by Factors Other Than the Preparation Program

Principal-preparation programs work to increase the odds that their graduates have desired characteristics. They do that by selecting candidates with the potential to attain those desired characteristics and by offering opportunities for them to enhance those characteristics. As noted by Grissom, Mitani, and Woo (2018), the relative contribution

---

[3] Grissom, Mitani, and Woo (2018) found that relationships between school outcomes and principal-preparation programs were not consistent across different outcome metrics for a set of principal-preparation programs in Tennessee.

of those two factors can be difficult to disentangle. Moreover, as time passes, graduates of principal-preparation programs have a number of other experiences in the workplace and elsewhere that are likely to influence their characteristics. Therefore, one must be careful in attributing characteristics that are observed in program graduates to the program activities alone.

These challenges argue for a nuanced examination of a range of outcomes and comparisons with outcomes of different groups that can shed light on how various aspects of a program contribute to outcomes. As illustrated in Figure 2.2, to influence school or student outcomes over the longer term, a program participant must complete the program, be hired as a principal, and then be retained as a principal after the first year. The yellow boxes in Figure 2.2 highlight the key milestones a candidate must achieve to have an effect on schools or students at all. This is true of comparison principals (i.e., those who attended non–New Leaders preparation programs) as well. For this reason, we consider whether graduates of New Leaders' Aspiring Principals program are placed as principals, whether they are retained as principals, and what outcomes they achieve as principals. If there are substantial differences among preparation programs in terms of placement or retention rates, that could influence how we think about the relative performance of these programs. When looking at the retention of newly placed principals in Tennessee, Grissom and Bartanen (2018) showed that high-performing principals—those who are rated highly by their supervisors and whose schools experience high achievement growth—have lower turnover than low-performing principals. They found that low-performing principals tended to return to teaching or to leave the education system entirely. They also found evidence suggesting that the highest performing principals are more likely to leave their schools because of promotion.

In addition, a district's propensity to make good hiring decisions will affect the extent to which both New Leaders and non–New Leaders principals are effective: Districts with high-quality recruiting processes are more likely than other districts to have effective principals in their schools, which, in turn, diminishes our ability to detect dif-

Figure 2.2
External Factors That Might Influence the Relationship Between New Leaders and School and Student Outcomes

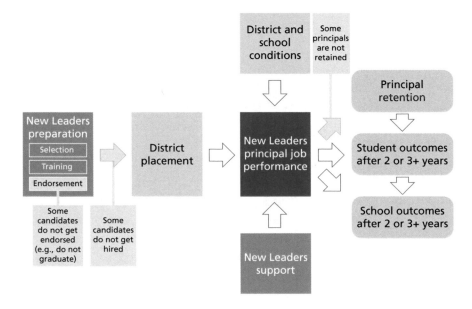

ferences in effectiveness between New Leaders and non–New Leaders principals.

The next chapter describes the methodological approaches we used to evaluate the Aspiring Principals program and address the analytical challenges stemming from potentially weak within-district contrast between New Leaders principals and other new principals within the same district.

CHAPTER THREE

Data and Methods

The focus of our study was the revised New Leaders' Aspiring Principals program, which was initially implemented in the 2012–2013 school year. We studied principals who had completed the Aspiring Principals program and participated in residencies in SY 2012–2013 through SY 2016–2017. We described these individuals and investigated whether schools and students led by these New Leaders principals outperformed comparison schools and students. We also looked at whether information gathered during the New Leaders program about the competencies of candidates was related to outcomes. In this chapter, we describe the data sources and analytic approaches we used to address the six research questions listed in Chapter One.

Definition of Treatment

To estimate program effects, we first specified what it means to be "treated" by the Aspiring Principals program intervention. We considered a school or student in participating districts to be treated by New Leaders' Aspiring Principals program if they had a New Leaders principal who was part of Cohorts 12–16. We identified schools with a New Leaders principal from earlier cohorts for certain sensitivity analyses and explorations, but these schools and students were not considered as "treated" in this analysis. In comparison were those schools in participating districts with a new principal who was not part of New Leaders' Aspiring Principals program. We included all New Leaders partner districts for which we had district-level data in the analysis.

Data

We collected a wide range of data over the course of the study. RAND's Institutional Review Board reviewed the collection and use of human-subjects data, such as student test scores or the characteristics of Aspiring Principals program participants. Additionally, the study established data-use agreements with New Leaders, with the help of the Utah Education Policy Center on behalf of the University Council for Educational Administration (UCEA) and participating states and districts, as required.

The data sources for our study were the following:

- **District data on students, schools, and principals:** New Leaders partner districts provided principal placement data and student demographic and outcome data from at least SY 2010–2011 through SY 2016–2017.
- **New Leaders program data:** RAND obtained data from New Leaders about Aspiring Principals program participants through SY 2016–2017 across 12 district sites.[1] These data included demographics, prior experience, assessment scores used for program admission, and assessment scores obtained during the Aspiring Principals program. We also determined whether the candidate was endorsed by New Leaders for principal placement. Measurements developed and employed in the New Leaders residency program were designed to capture residents' progress toward essential competencies. New Leaders organized these competencies into skill categories called *concepts* and into five broad standards. (See Appendix E for details.)
- **INSPIRE survey data:** RAND obtained data from surveys administered to residents during their residency year asking about their experiences during the residency, their assessments of those experiences, and their career aspirations. The most informative survey data were from the national INSPIRE survey, developed

---

[1]   These districts included the ten districts that were part of our broader analysis, plus two new partner districts that program participants were placed in.

and administered by the Utah Education Policy Center on behalf of the UCEA, which was completed by residents from Cohorts 13–16.

- **Interview and archival data:** Between 2013 and 2018, RAND interviewed representatives of eight of the 12 New Leaders partner districts included in our current evaluation at least twice. The interviews were conducted by phone, and RAND used a semistructured protocol that included open-ended questions regarding the district context, the principal's management practices, and the district's partnership with New Leaders. Specific questions varied by year. The protocol also included a series of closed-ended questions that asked participants to rate several aspects of the New Leaders partnership on a five-point scale—for example, *The partnership with New Leaders has benefited our district* and *New Leaders principals placed in our district in the last few years have been well prepared and of high quality.* We complemented our interview data with archival data that provided information about a district's context and its principal pipeline activities. We used these data to construct the district profiles included in Appendix A. The documents we reviewed varied by district and ranged from district websites and annual reports to newspaper articles about district activities and initiatives.

Overview of Approach

To address the research questions above, we used multiple methods. A key focus of this evaluation was a rigorous analysis of the outcomes of schools and students treated by the Aspiring Principals program through a New Leaders principal. We supplemented this analysis with a descriptive and exploratory evaluation of intermediate outcomes of interest, which also provided context for our findings. Table 3.1 briefly elaborates on each methodological approach and summarizes the relationship between these methods and the research questions. Detailed information about the methods used can be found in the appendixes.

Table 3.1
Approach Used to Address Research Questions

Research Question	Data and Methods Used
How do the outcomes of schools and students led by New Leaders principals compare with those of other schools and students in the district?	Analysis of program effects on school and student outcomes using New Leaders program data linked to district data
Are Aspiring Principals program graduates who are hired as principals in partner districts more or less likely to stay in their position than other new-principal hires?	Analysis of principal retention using New Leaders program data linked to district data
To what extent are Aspiring Principals program graduates being hired as principals in partner districts and in what types of schools?	Analysis of New Leaders program data linked to district data
What are the characteristics of the Aspiring Principals program participants?	Descriptive characterization drawn from New Leaders program data
To what extent are the competencies that the Aspiring Principals program participants demonstrate while they are in the program associated with placement as a principal, retention, and school or student outcomes?	Analysis of the relationships of principal characteristics and competencies to program effects on school and student outcomes using New Leaders program data linked to district data
How do Aspiring Principals program participants and partner districts view New Leaders and the Aspiring Principals program?	Descriptive characterization based on data from district interviews, the INSPIRE survey, and the New Leaders survey

Analysis of Program Participants and Their Assessed Performance

This analysis examined data that New Leaders gathered from Aspiring Principals program residents during the initial screening process and during enrollment in the program. These data included residents' demographic characteristics and prior work experiences and rich data about their competencies both before and during the program, as assessed by New Leaders. New Leaders measured principal attributes along five main standards: (1) Personal Leadership, (2) Instructional Leadership, (3) Cultural Leadership, (4) Adult and Team Leadership, and (5) Operational Leadership. These standards were divided into concepts, and concepts were further divided into specific observable competencies.

We analyzed data for 255 Aspiring Principals program participants who were residents in the 2012–2013, 2013–2014, 2014–2015, 2015–2016, or 2016–2017 school years across 12 district sites. The sample included all residents who participated in the program, regardless of whether they were successful in receiving New Leaders' endorsement at the conclusion of their program. We explored relationships between resident characteristics, including entry pathway, demographic characteristics, prior experience, and district context. We also examined data about the following intermediate outcomes:

- the Aspiring Principals program ratings
- the Aspiring Principals program ratings adjusted for pre-program ratings
- immediate placement as a principal upon graduation from the program.

We then explored whether these intermediate outcomes differed depending on a range of resident characteristics, including their entry pathway (i.e., whether they entered the program though the national recruitment and admissions process or the Emerging Leaders program); their gender, race, or ethnicity; their prior K–12 work experiences; and the city in which they took part in the Aspiring Principals program. We further considered a range of screening data, including assessment scores that influenced their entry into the Emerging Leaders program, and either national recruitment and admissions screening assessments or Emerging Leaders program assessments that influenced their entry into the Aspiring Principals program.

Analysis of Program Effects on Schoolwide Outcomes

In our first of two approaches to estimating the association between New Leaders principals and student outcomes, we used aggregated, school-level data to compare changes in average student attendance and performance on standardized reading and mathematics tests in treated schools with the same outcomes in comparison schools. This analysis attributed changes in student outcomes to the New Leaders principal, regardless of how long the students attended the school. A school is considered treated in years after a New Leaders principal is placed even if the principal leaves and is replaced by a principal not trained by New Leaders. Therefore, these results are akin to an "intent-to-treat" estimate of the association between New Leaders principals and student outcomes. This analysis of school-level "clusters" was conducted in a way that was consistent with the What Works Clearinghouse (WWC) guidelines for quasi-experimental studies and is expected to meet WWC evidence standards "with reservations."

In this section, we provide an overview of the analytic approach. Full technical details are available in Appendix B. As described in our pre-analysis plan, our primary outcomes of interest were results for all districts and cohorts three years after the initial placement of a New Leaders principal. Only the Aspiring Principals program graduates from Cohorts 12 and 13, who were placed as principals in SY 2013–2014 or 2014–2015, contributed to these estimates. Our focus on results three years after initial placement was grounded in research on the timing of the principal effect described in Chapter Two.

We identified a set of comparison schools through a propensity-matching approach. This approach matched schools in which New Leaders principals were newly hired to a group of control schools that (1) hired non–New Leaders principals the same year and (2) were comparable to the treated schools the year before the principal transition in terms of the outcome of interest.[2] We used these treatment schools and their matched control schools to calculate yearly estimates of the relationship between the New Leaders program and outcomes; we then generated a meta-analytic average of those estimates across all cohorts of principals, placing greater weight on the estimates that were more precise.

---

[2] Ideally, we would have matched on a pre-trend of the outcome variable; however, two of the nine districts did not provide data before 2013, the baseline year of the first cohort of New Leaders principals, making this approach infeasible. We also considered matching on a propensity score estimated with the three outcomes. This approach resulted in fewer schools available within a reasonable caliper. Ultimately, we chose to include those variables as controls after matching on the baseline outcome.

We employed two weighting strategies when pooling the results to answer two related, but distinct, research questions. The first strategy provided a school-level perspective by estimating the association between New Leaders principals and student outcomes in schools that hired a New Leaders principal. This strategy gave equal weight to each treatment school, so that those districts that placed more New Leaders principals had a greater influence on the results.[3] We referred to this strategy as the "school exposure" approach to weighting. The second strategy gave equal weight to outcomes for each district, regardless of the number of schools that hired New Leaders principals.[4] This weighting strategy estimated the association between New Leaders principals and student outcomes in the average district that placed New Leaders principals into their schools. We refer to this strategy as the "district average" approach to weighting. See Appendix B for more details on each weighting strategy.

We considered each weighting strategy to be a valid estimate of the effect of the New Leaders program, depending on the research question of interest. The two weighting strategies produced two estimates for each outcome domain. To avoid a type 1 error, we adjusted p-values for two hypothesis tests using the Benjamini-Hochberg correction, as recommended by the WWC (WWC, 2017).

We used this approach to analyze outcomes for K–8 schools because only about five New Leaders principals in our sample were placed into high schools in a given cohort, resulting in sample sizes by cohort that were too small to support the analytical approach. The prevalence of placement into K–8 schools is consistent with prior research examining the career paths into the high school principalship in North Carolina and Ohio. Burkhauser (2015) found that a vast majority of new high school principals were moving from a principalship in another school or from an assistant principalship. As a result, our findings should be

---

[3] Specifically, each treatment school is given a weight of 1.

[4] Specifically, the sum of the treatment weights is equal to 1 within each district. Therefore each treatment school receives a weight of $1/N_d$, where N_d is the number of treatment schools in a district. Control-school weights are also similarly transformed so that their sum always equals the treatment-school weight.

generalized only to elementary and middle schools in large urban districts and not necessarily to high schools; prior research has suggested that the nature of school leadership and the organizational challenges that face school leaders are different at the high school level (Pounder and Merrill, 2001; Copland and Boatright, 2006). For example, principals of elementary schools may be able to devote more time to hands-on instructional leadership, while principals of high schools may deal with more complex organizational challenges, operational issues, and requirements to distribute leadership across the school.

For each cohort of treated and comparison schools, we checked for baseline equivalence in each outcome of interest in the school year prior to the start of treatment.

This matching approach ensured baseline equivalence in the biggest predictor of the outcome of interest (the baseline measure of the outcome) and controlled for other key variables. Further, the difference-in-difference approach accounted for time-invariant characteristics of the school. With this method, however, as with all matching estimators, we were unable to ensure that all unobserved characteristics of the schools were accounted for. For example, if New Leaders principals were more likely to be placed in schools where student outcomes were trending downward above and beyond schools with similar baseline outcomes and student demographics—because the district thought these principals were more likely than other candidates to be successful in such schools—then our estimates would be biased downward. The opposite scenario is also possible. Similarly, if unobserved characteristics of the neighborhood or the resources available to the school were not fully accounted for by the baseline measure of the outcome and controls, our results may be biased. We view these results as robust associations estimated after accounting for the biggest predictors of outcomes.

Analysis of Program Effects on Individual Student Outcomes

The school-level analysis considered the effects a New Leaders principal had on a school overall, including those that arise from changes in the types of students attending that school before or after the new principal's arrival. A different question is whether New Leaders principals had a direct effect on individual students during the period these students attended schools led by those principals. We considered this question by looking at the change in outcomes of individual students who experienced both treated and untreated schools. We identify effects using students who moved from one school to another or who were in a school when a New Leaders principal joined or left. Such students may differ from student who do not experience such transitions, limiting the generalizability of our results. Although this methodological approach is rigorous, it does not follow a single, stable cohort of treatment and comparison schools or students. Also, it does not account for any effects that New Leaders principals may have on who chooses to attend their schools. Because of this, we present it as a supplement to the prior analysis of school-level impacts, which does follow a single, stable cohort of treatment and comparison schools. We provide an overview of the methodology here. A complete description is provided in Appendix C.

For the student-level analysis, we are able to evaluate effects for high school students, but we used somewhat different approaches to estimate effects for elementary and middle schools (K–8) to most effectively leverage the available data. When analyzing student achievement outcomes in elementary and middle schools, we used data from state-administered student tests in ELA and mathematics for grades 3–8 for all districts. We implemented a student fixed-effects estimator that relied on variation in outcomes for students during years when they were in schools with New Leaders principals versus years they were in schools not led by New Leaders principals.

The high school analysis (grades 9–12) differed because many districts administered the tests in only a single grade at that level, so we could not consistently use the student fixed-effects estimator. Instead, we included eighth grade test scores as a student-level control variable.

All models, examining both K–8 and high school outcomes, also controlled for school fixed effects and several demographic variables.

When New Leaders principals are placed in new schools with no previous data, we cannot control for school fixed effects for that specific school but can still control for student fixed effects. For all of these reasons, the sample of New Leaders principals that contributed to our findings in this methodology was similar, but not identical to, the sample of New Leaders principals in the analysis of schoolwide effects.

We estimated effects using the fixed-effects regressions for each district separately. We did this because data availability in regards to specific student and principal characteristics varied by district. We included as many relevant covariates as available in each district regression, as well as a control for principal tenure in the school and district. As for our analysis of New Leaders principals' effects on school-level outcomes, here too we explored two different approaches to averaging effects across districts. We considered both the simple average of effects across individual districts and an average effect that is weighted according to the number of our treated entities (in this case, students rather than schools) in each district.

We also investigated the impact of New Leaders principals on student attendance. We followed the same methodology as we did for student achievement in grades 2–8 (i.e., student and school fixed effects). Given attendance rates are observed for each grade in high school, as well as for preschool and first grade, we can follow the same methodology across all grade levels.

Analysis of Principal Retention

Given low principal retention rates and the high cost associated with principal training and onboarding (Miller, 2013; Goldring and Taie, 2014; School Leaders Network, 2014), our study examined the relationship between retention; participation in the New Leaders program; and principal, school, and district characteristics. We analyzed whether principals who experienced their first principal placement after the New Leaders program were more likely to remain in their principalship or in the district in the following years. As principals were not randomly assigned to schools, it is possible that New Leaders principals tended to be placed in either easier or more difficult school contexts. We controlled for observable school characteristics, including the racial and ethnic composition of the student body, the prior year's average mathematics and reading scores (standardized), and the school's structure (elementary, middle, or high school and school size), but these adjustments did not fully address the lack of random assignment, so causal interpretations of the resulting data should be made with caution.

We used linear probability models to analyze the retention of newly placed New Leaders principals and comparison principals. The analysis made use of administrative principal-placement data from New Leaders and panel data provided by nine districts; these data gave information about the principal in each school, for each year from 2013 to 2016, including the current principal. We used these data to construct our primary outcome measures: retention in position and retention in the district as a principal for two, three, and four years. Note that we could not observe the reason for failures in retention (i.e., departures may have been due to the principal wanting to leave or the district believing that another position was more suitable for the initially placed principal). We detected within-district moves to a principalship at another school for all principals, but for principals unaffiliated with New Leaders, we could not observe changes to other positions, such as a principal supervisory position or a district leadership position. We describe the data and approach in full detail in Appendix D and provide a brief overview here.

Analysis of the Relationship Between Outcomes and the Competency Measurements of Aspiring Principals Program Participants

While research has shown that some characteristics of principals are related to student outcomes (Grissom and Loeb, 2011; Grissom, Loeb, and Master, 2013)—characteristics that include supervisor ratings of principals (Grissom, Blissett, and Mitani, 2018)—researchers know relatively little about how to identify principal candidates who will be effective. Principal-preparation programs have an opportunity to measure candidates on several dimensions of practice and use those measurements to inform decisions about program progress and completion or determine whether to recommend the candidate for employment. Such use of program metrics would improve the quality of school leaders only if programs are able to identify, measure, and cultivate those knowledge areas and skills associated with improved student outcomes.

In this spirit, we analyzed whether New Leaders principals who were rated more highly on Aspiring Principals program measures had better retention rates and were associated with better improvements in attendance and achievement on state standardized reading and mathematics tests. We looked at relationships between New Leaders competency measures and outcomes and between New Leaders standards and outcomes. So that results were consistent across years, we used the 34 competencies that remained stable for Cohorts 13, 14, and 15. In all, the results encompassed 72 principals from those cohorts who were placed in partnering districts at any time between the 2014–2015 and 2016–2017 school years.

As discussed previously, Aspiring Principals program participants were measured on five broad standards during the course of the program. Each standard was composed of multiple competencies on which residents were rated. Some of the specific competencies measured varied year to year, with more substantial changes occurring prior to SY 2013–2014 (Cohort 13). To construct measures that would be comparable between years, we limited our analysis to Cohorts 13–15 of the Aspiring Principals program.

We conducted exploratory factor analysis at the competency level to identify groups of competencies that appeared closely related to one another.[5] This analysis identified three factors: Human Capital (composed of Standards 2 and 4), Cultural Capital (composed of Standards 3 and 5), and Personal Leadership (composed of Standard 1).

We then explored relationships between competencies and retention and other school outcomes. We used two approaches to address the challenge of relating school and student outcomes to principals' contributions, stemming from the fact that principals and students were not randomly assigned to schools. First, we employed "value-added" models that controlled for baseline academic achievement or student attendance levels. These value-added models were akin to those employed by Grissom, Kalogrides, and Loeb (2015) and Grissom, Blissett, and Mitani (2018). School value-added measures look at

---

[5]   Factor analysis was performed on the full sample of New Leaders principals. Factor scores of the analytical sample were used in the analysis.

the growth in test scores and account for observable student character-istics. In this way, we eliminated some of the bias that results from the nonrandom sorting of students to schools. We also controlled for stu-dent demographic data, including grade, indicators for having repeated a grade, race/ethnicity, gender, and English language learner (ELL) status, as well as school-level data, including the average characteristics of the student body and the size and type of school.

Second, when modeling the relationship between the Aspiring Principals program measures and the school value-added outcomes, we also controlled for the principal demographic characteristics as discussed in the data section. The principal demographics helped to account for any potential sorting of principals to schools based on observable characteristics.[6] Because there may be systematic differences in the labor market in each district we accounted for average differ-ences among districts. We also accounted for average differences in years of the outcome and in New Leaders principal cohorts. Finally, for all principals, we controlled for principals' baseline performance on similar measures from whichever pathway program they were recruited from so that results can be interpreted as growth in the measures. All standard errors were clustered by district.

We urge caution in attributing causal interpretation to our analy-ses correlating competencies with school outcomes. Because we lacked a research design that supports causal inferences for this research question, any relationship we observe might be attributable to other factors for which we were unable to control. For example, New Lead-ers principals who performed well in the training may be assigned to better-resourced (or worse-resourced) schools that might have higher (or lower) growth rates in student achievement and attendance regard-less of principal, thereby influencing the correlation between perfor-mance in the training and the effects on student achievement.

---

[6] Please see Appendix E for a discussion on controlling for principal baseline characteristics and pre-program ratings.

Analysis of INSPIRE Survey Data

We analyzed survey results from both INSPIRE surveys and New Leaders midyear surveys. The nationally normed INSPIRE survey was developed and administered by the Utah Education Policy Center on behalf of the UCEA, and data were available for four cohorts of the Aspiring Principals program residents (those in Cohorts 13, 14, 15, and 16). The midyear surveys were developed and administered by New Leaders, and data from that survey are available for five cohorts (Cohorts 12, 13, 14, 15, and 16). The INSPIRE survey asked graduates to provide an assessment of the quality of the program and of their learning outcomes. Program quality and learning outcomes questions were designed to assess the program's alignment with national standards for school leadership and with the characteristics of effective programs. Respondents were asked to rate their level of agreement with statements about the program on a five-point scale (1 = strongly disagree; 2 = disagree; 3 = neither agree nor disagree; 4 = agree; 5 = strongly agree). The INSPIRE survey questions were very similar from one year to the next. Although a few additional sections were added to the surveys administered to Cohorts 14, 15, and 16, we focused on those sections of the survey where the questions were consistent across years.

We examined descriptively how New Leaders' Aspiring Principals program residents rated their program on the INSPIRE survey. As an additional reference point, we also compared the INSPIRE survey results for the Aspiring Principals program residents to INSPIRE survey results from a national sample of principal leadership training program participants that attended UCEA member institutions (Pounder et al., 2016).

Qualitative Analysis of Interview and Archival Data

During our interviews with district officials, we took notes directly in the interview protocol document, and recorded the interviews to supplement the notes. The interview protocols were designed to gather information about the district context, including strategic priorities, budgetary constraints, and districtwide efforts related to the preparation, hiring, evaluation, and support of school leaders. The protocol also included questions about the district's partnership with New Leaders as an organization, as well as the role New Leaders and the principals trained by New Leaders plays in the district. Topics covered included goals and value of the partnership, perceptions of New Leaders' Aspiring Principals program graduates, and perceptions of New Leaders as a resource to the district and their value added. Condensed responses to each question were then entered into a spreadsheet to facilitate cross-district comparison. We looked across respondents' answers to identify themes and to examine district variability in responses. We examined the condensed notes and consulted the full notes, where appropriate, to summarize changes in each district. We used the interview data to share feedback with New Leaders throughout the project. In this report we used the data to provide an overview of how districts' goals for partnering with New Leaders changed over time.

We also used the interviews to complement the archival data we gathered to construct district profiles. More precisely, after reviewing the documents we gathered, we compared their information with the interview data to verify our findings. In line with our interview protocol design and objectives, the profiles found in Appendix A provide information about each district's (1) context during the New Leaders partnership, such as enrollment patterns, budgetary considerations, and strategic objectives; (2) goals for partnering with New Leaders; and (3) principal-pipeline activities, such as the development of leader standards, pre-service preparation programs, selective hiring and placement procedures, and principal support and evaluation. Nine of the ten profiles were sent to district officials to verify the information they contained, and any comments or corrections received were included in the final report. We were unable to contact district officials in New Orleans to verify that profile.

Study Limitations

The preparation, hiring, support, and retention of effective new principals is a complex, multistaged process that does not lend itself to a traditional experimental study design. To evaluate the effect of New

Leaders principals, we relied on quasi-experimental methods. There-fore, our evidence of causal effects should be interpreted with some cau-tion. Because aspiring principals were not randomly assigned to schools and students, it is possible that New Leaders principals were placed in schools that differed systematically—but in ways that we could not observe—from the schools into which non–New Leaders principals were placed. Such nonrandom sorting of principals to schools and stu-dents could have biased our estimates either positively or negatively. Moreover, since our analysis compared New Leaders principals with their peer novice principals in the same districts, our results are par-tially influenced by the districts' broader hiring, placement, and new-principal support efforts. Districts that are effective at hiring, plac-ing, and supporting new principals are likely to have less variation in the quality of newly placed principals. In turn, this would make it more difficult to identify differences among principals from differ-ent pre-service programs through within-district comparisons. The analysis relating Aspiring Principals program features to outcomes is exploratory in nature, and findings should not be interpreted as causal. Finally, our evaluation examines outcomes of graduates of a prepara-tion program with three core features, as described above. We were not able to modify the implementation of the program to test whether one or more of the core features of the Aspiring Principals program were more or less effective than others. As a result, we cannot comment on the relative value of any one feature or effective ways to modify the implementation of those features.

CHAPTER FOUR

Key Findings

In this chapter, we summarize our key findings related to each research question. The research questions and findings are aligned with the logic model presented in Chapter Two. We work backward from the outcomes in the logic model and then describe evidence that supports our hypotheses about how the program promoted those outcomes. More-detailed descriptions of analyses and findings are provided in separate appendixes related to each approach. Specifically, Appendix B details our analysis of schoolwide effects, Appendix C details our student-level analysis, Appendix D addresses our analysis of retention, and Appendix E summarizes our analysis relating principal competencies to school outcomes. Unless otherwise noted, we reference results as statistically significant if they are significant at the 5 percent level or lower.

How Did the Outcomes of Schools That Received a New Leaders Principal Compare with Those of Other Schools in the District That Received a New Principal Not Trained by New Leaders?

We found that New Leaders principals were positively associated with school-level student achievement. Table 4.1 shows the pooled results of the effect of New Leaders principals on schools' student outcomes three years after hiring. These were the average effects of New Leaders principals trained in Cohort 12 and later who were later hired in K–8 schools in SY 2013–2014 and SY 2014–2015. Panel A illustrates

Table 4.1
Meta-Analytic Averages of the Effect of New Leaders Principals on Student Outcomes in K–8 Schools, by Weighting Strategy

	(1) Mathematics	(2) ELA	(3) Attendance
Panel A: Weighted by treatment schools per district			
New Leaders effect after 3 years	0.089* (0.029)	0.057* (0.025)	0.004 (0.003)
New Leaders effect after 3 years (percentile points)	3.55* (1.20)	2.27* (1.00)	N/A
p-value	0.003	0.024	0.151
Benjamini-Hochberg threshold	0.025	0.025	0.025
Panel B: Equal weight for each district			
New Leaders effect after 3 years	0.082* (0.029)	0.045 (0.025)	0.003 (0.003)
New Leaders effect after 3 years (percentile points)	3.26* (1.18)	1.81 (1.01)	N/A
p-value	0.006	0.074	0.400
Benjamini-Hochberg threshold	0.050	0.050	0.050
N (schools)	226	240	152

NOTES: N/A = not applicable. Standard errors are in parentheses. The meta-analytic averages combine the effects of principals placed in SY 2013–2014 and SY 2014–2015. The individual cohort estimates were calculated using nearest-neighbor matching with replacement, with a caliper of a 0.25 standard deviation of the outcome variable at baseline. Two weights were calculated. The first gives each treatment school a weight of 1 and the second weights each treatment school such that their sum equals 1 in a district. In addition to matching weights, cohort-specific models include baseline measures of all outcome variables, an indicator for ever being led by a New Leaders principal trained before Cohort 12, a continuous measure of principal tenure, and an indicator for new principals. Standard errors in cohort-specific models were clustered by school. The meta-analytic average includes fixed effects and employed the inverse of the variance of the cohort estimate as weights. Mathematics and ELA results are presented in effect-size units and percentage points. Attendance results are presented in percentage points.

* Indicates the significance is robust to the Benjamini-Hochberg correction for two-hypotheses tests.

the results weighted by the number of treatment schools. These results indicated that New Leaders principals were associated with an increase in student achievement in mathematics by a significant 0.09 standard deviation (a 3.55 percentile gain) and an increase in achievement in ELA by a significant 0.06 standard deviation (a 2.27 percentile gain). In each case, percentile gains indicate how much higher an average student would be expected to perform (e.g., going from the 50th percentile in mathematics to the 53rd percentile) as a result of being in a school led by a New Leaders principal. We did not detect a statistically significant association with attendance using this model. Panel B shows that when weighting each district equally, a significant association with mathematics achievement—a 0.08 standard deviation or a 3.26 percentile gain—remained, but the point estimate for ELA achievement was reduced to a 0.05 standard deviation and was not significant. Once again, there was no discernible association with attendance.

The pattern of results across weighting approaches suggested that districts that placed more New Leaders principals saw slightly larger achievement levels, though the point estimates between panels A and B were not significantly different from each other. All levels of significance reported are robust to a Benjamini-Hochberg multiple-hypothesis testing correction for our two comparisons per domain. Without this correction, the 0.05 standard deviation increase in ELA achievement when weighting each district equally was significant to the 10 percent level.

To ensure that our primary analysis of program impacts on school-level outcomes could meet the highest WWC evidence standards for a quasi-experimental study, we checked for baseline equivalence in the outcome of interest for each cohort. Across all estimates weighted by cohort outcome, no baseline measure was significantly imbalanced across treatment and control schools. Please see Table B.1 for all cohort-specific estimates of baseline equivalence. Though none of the baseline differences exceeded the WWC limit of a 0.25 standard deviation (and few were above a 0.05 standard deviation), our models controlled for baseline outcomes through propensity score matching to produce doubly robust estimates; doing so would account for any lingering bias in baseline outcomes that the matching process did not fully account for. Table 4.2 shows the meta-analytic baseline equivalence estimates. None exceeds a 0.05 standard deviation.

Sample sizes for the school-level analysis presented in Tables 4.1 and 4.2 represent the number of schools contributing to the analysis. We confirmed that the students contributing to the school-level estimates were representative of the students who were in the school as a whole (see Appendix Table B.4). The proportion of eligible students who had valid outcomes ranged from 90 percent to 96 percent, depending on cohort, and from 92 percent to 94 percent for students contributing to the meta-analytic average. The representativeness of all samples fell well within the bounds put forth by the WWC (WWC, 2017).

How Did the Outcomes of Students with a New Leaders Principal Compare with Those of Other Students in the District?

In this section, we describe findings from our analysis to address the question, What is the impact on a student of attending a school led by a New Leaders principal? Readers are referred to Appendix C for a full description of the results. We used data from the 2012–2013 school year to the 2016–2017 school year. We used all cohorts of New Lead-

Table 4.2
Meta-Analytic Averages of Baseline Differences in K–8 Schools, by Weighting Method

	(1) Mathematics	(2) ELA	(3) Attendance
Weighted by treatment schools	−0.014 (0.026)	−0.008 (0.025)	0.000 (0.002)
Equal weights to districts	−0.003 (0.025)	−0.003 (0.023)	0.000 (0.002)
N (schools)	226	240	152

NOTE: Meta-analytic averages are calculated using fixed effects and the inverse of the variance as weights.

ers principals who completed their residency after SY 2011–2012. We analyzed outcomes for elementary and middle school students separately from those of high school students. This approach to estimating the relationship between New Leaders principals and student outcomes identified effects based on those students who spent time both in and out of New Leaders schools in different school years. While rigorous, this analysis differs from our prior analysis of schoolwide effects in that it is not an approach that meets the current WWC evidence standards.

Appendix Table B.1 presents the summary statistics for our sample.

Elementary and Middle School Results

We found a positive and statistically significant relationship between exposure to a New Leaders principal with three or more years of experience (see Appendix Tables C.1 and C.2). These results were positive and large (around a 3 to 5 percentile increase), and they were statistically significant for both subjects using the district-average approach to weighting. These results were larger than the findings in our 2014 study, which associated New Leaders principals with achievement gains of 1.3 percentile points in mathematics and 0.7 percentile points in ELA. The relationship between three years of exposure to a New Leaders principal and outcomes is moderately sized for mathematics using the school approach to weighting but is not statistically significant. Although not presented here, we found the first-year effects to be universally negative, although only statistically significantly negative for reading using the school-exposure approach to weighting. The point estimates for the first-year effects were small in all cases. These patterns suggest that the effects became more positive with more years of principal experience in a school, resulting in positive effects by the third year. Again, these patterns are similar to those we found in our prior evaluation of New Leaders (Gates et al., 2014a).

At the elementary and middle school levels, we found that having a New Leaders principal was associated with better attendance outcomes, when using the equal-weighted average. The relationship was statistically significant and positive for the first, second, and third years after placement and later. The average effect for elementary and middle schools was an attendance rate between 0.1 and 0.7 percentage points higher, which equates to between approximately 0.2 and 1.25 school days per year.

High School Results

With a small sample size, our analysis found few statistically significant relationships between New Leaders principals and outcomes at the high school level. This could be because our methodology and sample size did not have sufficient power to detect an effect or because there was no effect at the high school level. We found some statistically significant effects that were based on findings from a small number of Aspiring Principals program graduates placed in high schools. We found a positive and statistically significant relationship between exposure to a New Leaders principal with three or more years of experience (see Appendix Table C.2) and ELA achievement using the district-average weighting approach. These effects are large, with an increase of greater than 9 percentile points. However, the relationships were not significant when using the school-average approach to weighting.

The patterns in the high school results were consistent with the findings from our 2014 study, where the only statistically significant relationship observed was between exposure to a New Leaders principal at the high school level with three or more years of experience and improved reading achievements of 3 percentile points (Gates et al., 2014a). It was in the 2014 study where we also observed substantial variation by district.

We found a negative and statistically significant relationship between exposure to a New Leaders principal with three or more years of experience (see Appendix Table C.5) and attendance using the district-average approach to weighting. Students in schools led by a New Leaders principal had attendance rates almost 2 percentage points lower than students in non–New Leaders schools. The estimate using the school-weighted average was also negative but not statistically significant. Exploratory analyses suggested that exposure to New Leaders principals with one or two years of experience may also be associated with lower attendance.

Were the Aspiring Principals Program Graduates Hired as Principals in Partner Districts More or Less Likely to Stay in Their Position Compared with Other New-Principal Hires?

To address this question, we analyzed the retention rates of newly placed principals in New Leaders partner districts. We defined *retention* as holding principalship in the same school for two or three years. We found that after controlling for school characteristics, newly placed New Leaders principals were, on average, across districts and across cohorts, approximately 8 percentage points more likely to remain in their position for a second year ($p < 0.01$) than other newly placed principals in the same district. There was no statistically significant difference between New Leaders and non–New Leaders in terms of their propensity to stay in their schools for at least three years. The sign and strength of the relationship between New Leaders principals and retention varied by district.

To What Extent Did Partner Districts Hire Aspiring Principals Program Graduates and in What Types of Schools?

Between the 2013–2014 and 2017–2018 school years, 350 new Aspiring Principals program graduates were hired by partner districts in educational positions. Of those, 129 (37 percent) were initially hired as principals and 159 (45 percent) hired as assistant principals. Another 49 (14 percent) were hired in supervisory or district roles, and three (less than 1 percent) returned to teaching. The remainder were placed in other school-affiliated positions. By their third year after program completion, 195 (56 percent) Aspiring Principals program graduates had served as principals, and 318 (91 percent) had served as either an assistant principal or a principal. Principal hiring rates varied across districts, probably in part because of differences in district policies. Within districts, we found no evidence that the pathway through which residents were recruited (either the national recruitment and admissions process or the Emerging Leaders program) was related to placement.

As indicated in Table 4.3, rates for immediate principal placement ranged from 26.2 percent for Cohort 16 graduates to 39.3 percent for Cohort 15 graduates. Taking a longer view, however, two-thirds of Cohort 12 graduates had been hired as a principal within five years of completing the program. These hiring outcomes are substantially higher than placement rates reported in a recent study of several principal-preparation programs based on an analysis of administrative data from the state of Tennessee. Specifically, Grissom, Mitani, and Woo (2018) found that, across ten principal-preparation programs in that state, rates for principal placement (measured from the time the licensure exam was taken) varied between 6 percent and 17 percent.

Figure 4.1 presents the estimated difference between baseline characteristics (that is, characteristics of the school's student population in the year prior to placement) of schools with newly hired New Leaders principals and those of the district average. New Leaders principals were hired in schools that tended to have lower-achieving students, a greater fraction of minority students, and more students eligible for the free and reduced-price lunch program. However, in all cases, the difference was less than 1 standard deviation of the result in the district. Also, although not shown in Table 4.3, there was no systematic difference between schools led by New Leaders principals and the district in terms of ELL students or school type (elementary, middle, or high school). Appendix Table B.6 presents the averages for the New Leaders schools and the districts.

What Characteristics Did the Aspiring Principals Program Participants Possess and Which Were Associated with Assessed Performance in the Program and Placement After Graduation?

Table 4.3 provides a descriptive overview of the Aspiring Principals program participants who completed the program.[1] Of the five Aspir-

---

[1]   We obtained data only for those who completed the program. According to New Leaders data, over 90 percent of those who start the program complete it. In Cohort 12, 94 partici-

Figure 4.1
Difference in Student Characteristics for New Leaders Schools Compared with All District Schools

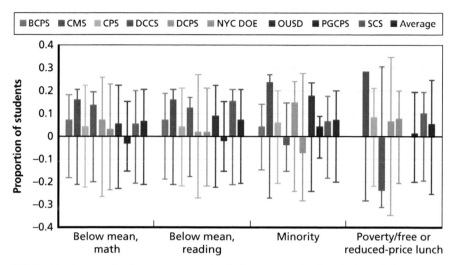

NOTES: For frame of reference, we also include a ±1 standard deviation of the same measure in the whiskers. BCPS = Baltimore City Public Schools; CMS = Charlotte-Mecklenburg Schools; CPS = Chicago Public Schools; DCCS = D.C. charter schools; DCPS = District of Columbia Public Schools; NYC DOE = New York City Department of Education; OUSD = Oakland Unified School District; PGCPS = Prince George's County Public Schools; SCS = Shelby County Schools.

ing Principals program cohorts (Cohorts 12, 13, 14, 15, and 16 from SY 2012–2013, SY 2013–2014, SY 2014–2015, SY 2015–2016, and SY 2016–2017, respectively), Cohorts 12, 13, and 14 included comparable numbers of residents, with between 78 and 90 residents, while Cohorts 15 and 16 were smaller, with 61 and 65 residents. Across cohorts, nearly three-quarters of residents were women, and over half were non-white. A majority of the residents in each cohort entered Aspiring Principals via the Emerging Leaders program pathway, and in Cohorts 13, 14, and 15, Emerging Leaders entrants represented more than two-thirds of the total. As indicated in the chart, there were no New Leaders residents in Charlotte after Cohort 13 and in Prince George's County after Cohort 14, although the districts continued to

---

pants started and 87 completed the program. In Cohort 13, 96 started and 90 completed. In Cohort 14, all participants completed the program.

Table 4.3
Descriptive Statistics for New Leaders Residents, by Aspiring Principals Program Cohort

Characteristics and experiences	Cohort 12 (SY 2012–2013)		Cohort 13 (SY 2013–2014)		Cohort 14 (SY 2014–2015)		Cohort 15 (SY 2015–2016)		Cohort 16 (SY 2016–2017)	
	%	Fraction	%	Fraction	%	Fraction	%	Fraction	%	Fraction
White	36.7	(29/79)	29.1	(25/86)	34.7	(26/75)	26.4	(14/53)	31.3	(20/64)
Black	48.1	(38/79)	52.3	(45/86)	52.0	(39/75)	54.7	(29/53)	48.4	(31/64)
Hispanic	7.6	(6/79)	14.0	(12/86)	5.3	(4/75)	7.5	(4/53)	14.1	(9/64)
Other race/multiracial	7.6	(6/79)	4.7	(4/86)	8.0	(6/75)	11.3	(6/53)	6.3	(4/64)
Female	71.6	(58/81)	76.1	(67/88)	72.7	(56/77)	78.2	(43/55)	73.8	(48/65)
National recruitment and admissions (vs. Emerging Leaders) pathway	46.0	(40/87)	33.3	(30/90)	28.2	(22/78)	27.9	(17/61)	43.1	(28/65)
Emerging Leaders program "pass" at entry (Emerging Leaders only)	N/A[a]	N/A[a]	50.8	(31/61)	63.2	(36/57)	52.6	(20/38)	78.8	(26/33)
Endorsed by New Leaders	96.6	(84/87)	94.4	(85/90)	94.9	(74/78)	93.4	(57/61)	92.3	(60/65)
Placement as a principal to date	66.7	(58/87)	52.2	(47/90)	56.4	(44/78)	50.8	(31/61)	26.2	(17/65)
Immediate principal placement	39.1	(34/87)	35.6	(32/90)	37.2	(29/78)	39.3	(24/61)	26.2	(17/65)

Table 4.3—Continued

	Cohort 12 (SY 2012–2013)		Cohort 13 (SY 2013–2014)		Cohort 14 (SY 2014–2015)		Cohort 15 (SY 2015–2016)		Cohort 16 (SY 2016–2017)	
	%	Fraction	%	Fraction	%	Fraction	%	Fraction	%	Fraction
Sites										
Baltimore	10.3	(9/87)	8.9	(8/90)	11.5	(9/78)	16.4	(10/61)	15.4	(10/65)
Bay Area	5.7	(5/87)	10.0	(9/90)	14.1	(11/78)	18.0	(11/61)	13.8	(9/65)
Charlotte	11.5	(10/87)	10.0	(9/90)	0.0	(0/78)	0.0	(0/61)	0.0	(0/65)
Chicago	26.4	(23/87)	30.0	(27/90)	37.2	(29/78)	27.9	(17/61)	27.7	(18/65)
Memphis	8.0	(7/87)	6.7	(6/90)	9.0	(7/78)	11.5	(7/61)	16.9	(11/65)
New Orleans	3.4	(3/87)	4.4	(4/90)	3.8	(3/78)	3.3	(2/61)	0.0	(0/65)
New York	10.3	(9/87)	12.2	(11/90)	10.3	(8/78)	4.9	(3/61)	6.2	(4/65)
Newark	1.1	(1/87)	1.1	(1/90)	1.3	(1/78)	6.6	(4/61)	1.5	(1/65)
Prince George's County	10.3	(9/87)	7.8	(7/90)	5.1	(4/78)	0.0	(0/61)	0.0	(0/65)
Washington, D.C.	12.6	(11/87)	8.9	(8/90)	7.7	(6/78)	8.2	(5/61)	12.3	(8/65)

[a] Not applicable. The Emerging Leaders program pathway started with Cohort 13.

hire New Leaders principals trained in earlier cohorts. Although not reported in Table 4.3, we also looked at whether Aspiring Principals program candidates identified through the national recruitment and admissions pathway were local to the partner district, meaning that they resided in the area at the time they applied for the program. New Leaders' program data indicated that, for Cohorts 12 through 16, this pathway was drawing primarily but not exclusively from the local area. Nationally, 8 percent of candidates were outside the local area at the time they applied to the program. The prevalence of out-of-area candidates ranged from a high of 28 percent in Charlotte to 0 in Prince George's County and San Antonio.

We used a variety of data collected by New Leaders to better understand variation in the assessed performance of individuals in the program. Aspiring Principals program participants were rigorously screened prior to entering the program, either through intensive interviews conducted as part of the national recruitment and admissions pathway or through a more gradual process as part of the Emerging Leaders program. Subsequently, during the Aspiring Principals program, participants were evaluated regularly with respect to their knowledge, skills, and abilities. We analyzed which resident characteristics were associated with higher performance ratings in the Aspiring Principals program, as well as the relationships between pre-screening ratings from the national recruitment and admissions process and the Emerging Leaders program and subsequent performance during residency. We also explored the extent to which assessed performance varied across districts. This section highlights our key findings from this analysis.[2]

We found that ratings of applicants before their entry into the Aspiring Principals program were a consistent and highly significant predictor of their performance in the program. The effect size was modest, however, with a pre–Aspiring Principals program rating of 1 standard deviation higher corresponding to in-program ratings of anywhere from 0.13 to 0.18 standard deviations higher. The relationship

---

[2]   In the interest of brevity, we do not include full tables of the results related to predicting Aspiring Principals program ratings. Complete results tables are available upon request.

between pre-program and in-program ratings was statistically significant for applicants from both the national recruitment and admissions and Emerging Leaders program pathways. This finding suggests that New Leaders was similarly accurate in evaluating residents as part of the shorter national recruitment and admissions pathway recruitment process as it was when evaluating candidates through the lengthy Emerging Leaders program process.

We also found that, among residents, women scored significantly higher than men in the Aspiring Principals program ratings. This was particularly true in the areas of Instructional Leadership and Adult and Team Leadership. In the former, female residents scored 0.35 standard deviations higher than their male counterparts (roughly equivalent to the difference between rating in the 50th and the 64th percentiles); in the latter, female residents scored 0.30 standard deviations higher. Findings were similar for analyses that controlled for pre–Aspiring Principals program ratings. The consistency of the results for pre–Aspiring Principals program ratings, with or without controls, offers some evidence that differences in the Aspiring Principals program ratings may be related to actual program effects on female residents' performance and not just to preexisting differences in candidates' abilities.

A variety of other resident characteristics—including race/ethnicity, years of prior teaching experience, and the pathway by which residents were recruited into the Aspiring Principals program (through either the Emerging Leaders program or the national recruitment and admissions process)—were not significantly associated with Aspiring Principals program ratings, with or without controls for pre–Aspiring Principals program ratings. Residents who worked in a school led by former Aspiring Principals program graduates scored significantly lower in the Aspiring Principals program ratings. However, this association disappears when controlling for pre–Aspiring Principals program ratings, which suggests that while these residents were assessed as lower-performing, they showed comparable rates of learning when taking into account their ratings before starting the program. Finally, we found that the ratings that mentor principals in the residency schools gave to the overall residency program design were strongly associated with the ratings that residents received from Aspiring Principals program staff. It is unclear, however, whether this is because mentors thought better of the program when their residents performed better, or if it was because residents performed better when the residency program at their school was, in fact, better managed.

Across districts, Aspiring Principals program ratings varied substantially, though it is unclear whether this variation stemmed from differences in performance levels or rating practices. Typically, site-level ratings were better (or worse) than average across multiple individual standards. Analyses that controlled for variation in the Aspiring Principals program ratings across sites yielded similar findings to the analyses without district fixed effects included as controls. In other words, the Aspiring Principals program ratings were similarly predictive of or correlated with pre–Aspiring Principals program ratings regardless of whether average Aspiring Principals program scores differed across individual sites.

Finally, we examined whether Aspiring Principals program participant ratings or characteristics predicted variation in their immediate hiring as principals following graduation from the program. We found that ratings were highly predictive of immediate placement rates. Other resident characteristics, including gender, race, entry pathway, and years of prior teaching, were generally not significantly associated with immediate placement rates. The relationship between higher Aspiring Principals program ratings and higher immediate placement rates was consistent when controlling for variation in placement rates at each of the individual sites. These results suggest that residents with higher program ratings were more attractive on the job market or that New Leaders and participating districts were more successful in steering higher-rated residents toward placement as principals.

To What Extent Are Aspiring Principals Program Participants' Competencies Associated with Retention and School or Student Outcomes?

Aspiring Principals program residents were assessed on five broad standards while in the program: (1) Personal Leadership, (2) Instructional Leadership, (3) Cultural Leadership, (4) Adult and Team Leadership, and (5) Operational Leadership. Each standard comprised several competencies. A factor analysis done at the competency level suggested three constructs into which competencies could be grouped: Human Capital (composed of Standards 2 and 4), Cultural Capital (composed of Standards 3 and 5), and Personal Leadership (composed of Standard 1). Overall, we found that the Human Capital construct, including Standards 2 and 4, is most robustly related to student attendance and achievement in mathematics and ELA, while the Cultural Capital construct, encompassing Standards 3 and 5, were most robustly related to principal retention.

Table 4.4 illustrates the relationships between the constructs underlying the competency measures, standards, and student academic and attendance outcomes.[3] Panel A presents the underlying construct results. Construct 1, the Human Capital construct, was the one most robustly associated with student outcomes. An increase of 1 standard deviation in this construct was associated with a 0.035 standard deviation increase in ELA performance (1.38 percentile points; $p < 0.01$), a 0.045 standard deviation increase in mathematics performance (1.79 percentile points; $p < 0.05$), and a 0.5 percentage point increase in attendance (an increase of 0.9 of a day in attendance; $p < 0.05$). Meanwhile, the Cultural Capital construct was not significantly related to any student outcome, with all point estimates small and insignificant. Similarly, the Personal Leadership construct was related only to mathematics achievement. An increase of 1 standard deviation in the Personal Leadership construct was related to a 0.016 standard deviation decrease in mathematics achievement (−0.1633 percentile points; $p < 0.05$). In each case, percentile points indicated how far students were expected to move up (or down) the distribution of scores as a result of the relationships with each construct. For example, the 1.38 percentile increase in ELA associated with a 1 standard deviation increase in the

---

[3]   All models control for pre-program measures administered by the Emerging Leaders program and national recruitment and admissions recruitment pathways. These pre-program measures are aligned with, but not strictly analogous to, the residency program measures. Their inclusion controls for a rough measure of baseline ability in the New Leader. Results do not appreciably change when excluding this control. Please see Appendix E for details.

Table 4.4
Relationship Between Aspiring Principals Program Competency Measures and Student Outcomes

	(1) ELA	(2) Mathematics	(3) Attendance
Panel A: Underlying competency constructs			
Construct 1 (Human Capital)	0.035*** (0.010)	0.045** (0.014)	0.005** (0.002)
Construct 2 (Cultural Capital)	−0.003 (0.011)	−0.022 (0.016)	0.003 (0.002)
Construct 3 (Personal Leadership)	−0.004 (0.014)	−0.016** (0.006)	0.000 (0.002)
Panel B: Standards (in separate regressions)			
Standard 1 (Personal Leadership)	0.004 (0.015)	−0.010 (0.008)	0.003 (0.003)
Standard 2 (Instructional Leadership)	0.025* (0.012)	0.028* (0.014)	0.006** (0.002)
Standard 3 (Cultural Leadership)	0.010 (0.012)	0.004 (0.011)	0.003 (0.002)
Standard 4 (Adult and Team Leadership)	0.044** (0.017)	0.030** (0.012)	0.005 (0.003)
Standard 5 (Operational Leadership)	0.024 (0.018)	0.012 (0.012)	0.004 (0.003)
Baseline ELA and mathematics scores	X	X	
Baseline attendance			X
Pre–Aspiring Principals program scores	X	X	X
New Leaders principal covariates	X	X	X
Student covariates	X	X	X
School covariates	X	X	X
Cohort fixed effects	X	X	X
Year fixed effects	X	X	X

Table 4.4—Continued

	(1) ELA	(2) Mathematics	(3) Attendance
District fixed effects	X	X	X
Observations	28,489	28,489	51,803

NOTES: Standard errors are clustered at the school level. New Leaders principal covariates include pre-residency recruitment pathways, an indicator for passing the Emerging Leaders program screening, years of experience as a teacher, gender, race/ethnicity, an indicator for the residency occurring in a charter school, and an indicator for the residency occurring in a school led by a New Leader from a previous cohort. Student covariates include fixed effects for grade, an indicator for having repeated a grade, ELL classification, race/ethnicity, gender, and an indicator for being old for the grade. School covariates include school enrollment, school level, and school-level averages of race/ethnicity, gender, ELL classification, students repeating a grade, and students old for their grade. Constructs were made via a factor analysis of the underlying competency data.

* $p < 0.1$, ** $p < 0.05$, *** $p < 0.01$.

Human Capital construct is equivalent to moving students from the 50th percentile to just above the 51st percentile.

Panel B presents relationships between New Leaders' standards measures and outcomes. Standards 2 (Instructional Leadership) and 4 (Adult and Team Leadership) showed the greatest association with outcomes. Standard 2 was marginally significantly related to ELA and mathematics achievement, by 0.025 and 0.028 standard deviations (0.99 and 1.10 percentile points), and significantly associated with attendance by 0.6 percentage points (one additional day of attendance; $p < 0.05$). Meanwhile, Standard 4 significantly increased ELA and mathematics achievement by 0.044 and 0.03 standard deviations (1.76 and 1.19 percentile points; $p < 0.05$). Though the point estimate on attendance was positive, it was not significant. In contrast, Standard 1 (Personal Leadership), Standard 3 (Cultural Leadership), and Standard 5 (Operational Leadership) on their own were not significantly associated with any student outcomes. These results were consistent with the construct results where only Construct 1, composed of Standards 2 and 4, was robustly associated with student outcomes. To provide more context, the Instructional Leadership standard was composed of measures of pedagogical and instructional leadership, data-driven instruction, observation and supervision of instruction, standards-based planning, and curriculum assessment. Adult and Team Leadership was composed of performance management measures, leadership development, and professional development of building staff.

We also analyzed the relationship between the New Leaders constructs and standards and principal retention (see Table 4.5). All standards other than Instructional Leadership were significantly related ($p < 0.10$) to two-year in-position and in-district retention; however, there is much commonality among these standards. Looking at competencies, we found that neither the Human Capital construct nor the Personal Leadership construct was significantly related to retention in the principalship. The Cultural Capital construct strongly relates to in-district and in-position retention, although this relationship is weakened slightly by district fixed effects. An increase of 1 standard deviation in this construct raised the probability of retention by between 7 and 10 percentage points.

How Do Aspiring Principals Program Participants and Partner Districts View New Leaders and the Aspiring Principals Program?

Perspectives of Aspiring Principals Program Participants

As noted in Chapter Three, the INSPIRE survey was developed and administered by the Utah Education Policy Center on behalf of the UCEA and made data available for the Aspiring Principals program residents in Cohorts 13, 14, 15, and 16. We descriptively compared INSPIRE survey scores across all four Aspiring Principals program cohorts with a national sample of principal-training program participants (Pounder et al., 2016). We focused our analysis on a large portion of the survey (nine sections in total), repeated all four years, which provided responses from Aspiring Principals program residents. In addition, while results from all four cohorts are potentially of interest, when conducting statistical tests directly comparing Aspiring Principals with the national sample, we limited our sample to the single school year (2015–2016) in which both groups took the identical survey.

Table 4.5
Relationship Between Aspiring Principals Program Competency Measures and Principal-Retention Outcomes

	(1)	(2)	(3)	(4)
	Same Position in Year 2		Same District in Year 2	
Panel A: Constructs of underlying competencies				
Construct 1 (Human Capital)	0.0475	0.0582	0.0261	0.0259
	(0.0559)	(0.0683)	(0.0341)	(0.0291)
Construct 2 (Cultural Capital)	0.0928**	0.0807*	0.100***	0.0933***
	(0.0407)	(0.0467)	(0.0249)	(0.0199)
Construct 3 (Personal Leadership)	0.0208	0.0349	0.0275	0.0167
	(0.0486)	(0.0623)	(0.0296)	(0.0266)
Panel B: Standards (in separate regressions)				
Standard 1 (Personal Leadership)	0.128**	0.137*	0.135***	0.133**
	(0.0602)	(0.0714)	(0.0470)	(0.0513)
Standard 2 (Instructional Leadership)	0.0690	0.0675	0.0524	0.0452
	(0.0716)	(0.0860)	(0.0588)	(0.0651)
Standard 3 (Cultural Leadership)	0.105*	0.109	0.117**	0.109*
	(0.0604)	(0.0777)	(0.0475)	(0.0569)
Standard 4 (Adult and Team Leadership)	0.110	0.111	0.112*	0.120*
	(0.0690)	(0.0874)	(0.0552)	(0.0638)
Standard 5 (Operational Leadership)	0.0928	0.137*	0.102*	0.141**
	(0.0725)	(0.0780)	(0.0582)	(0.0557)
New Leaders principal covariates	X	X	X	X
District fixed effects		X		X
Observations	35	35	35	35

NOTES: New Leaders principal covariates are indicators for African American, Hispanic, and female. Constructs were made via factor analysis of the underlying competency data.

* $p < 0.1$, ** $p < 0.05$, *** $p < 0.01$.

Residents' responses on the INSPIRE survey were overwhelmingly positive in all sections and were fairly consistent across cohorts (see Table 4.6). Their average program ratings (on a five-point Likert scale) were equivalent to or higher than ratings given by other principal-

Table 4.6
INSPIRE Survey Results: Mean Ratings of Aspiring Principals Program Residents, by Cohort and Survey Section

Sample (N)	Rigor and Relevance		Faculty Quality		Peer Relationships		Program Accessibility and Attractiveness		Internship Design and Quality		Organization and School Culture		Instructional Leadership		Management		Family and Community Relations	
	Mean	Std. Dev.	Mean	Std. Dev.	Mean	Std. Dev.	Mean	Std. Dev.	Mean	Std. Dev.	Mean	Std. Dev.	Mean	Std. Dev.	Mean	Std. Dev.	Mean	Std. Dev.
Cohorts 13–14 (N = 86)	4.50	(0.45)	4.51	(0.53)	4.55	(0.55)	4.31	(0.53)	4.42	(0.61)	4.51	(0.51)	4.49	(0.56)	4.00	(0.81)	4.29	(0.60)
Cohorts 14–15 (N = 55)	4.69	(0.42)	4.69	(0.48)	4.72	(0.45)	4.41	(0.45)	4.60	(0.50)	4.74	(0.41)	4.66	(0.42)	4.31	(0.67)	4.61	(0.52)
Cohorts 15–16 (N = 51)	4.71**	(0.33)	4.77**	(0.34)	4.71***	(0.45)	3.93**	(0.56)	4.42	(0.58)	4.60	(0.41)	4.63***	(0.43)	4.18	(0.57)	4.43	(0.42)
Cohorts 16–17 (N = 49)	4.52	(0.29)	4.51	(0.32)	4.48	(0.38)	4.42	(0.34)	4.56	(0.30)	4.43	(0.40)	4.44	(0.37)	4.35	(0.38)	4.40	(0.43)
National sample (UCEA) (N = 726)	4.44	(0.64)	4.55	(0.60)	4.21	(0.86)	4.17	(0.60)	4.24	(0.85)	4.44	(0.59)	4.21	(0.71)	4.03	(0.78)	4.32	(0.71)

NOTES: Data are given for only those sections repeated in all years of survey administration. Information for the UCEA national sample is from the 2016 INSPIRE survey. Significance tests shown are for results of t-tests comparing Cohort 15–16 responses on each survey section with UCEA national sample responses.

$* p < 0.1$, $** p < 0.05$, $*** p < 0.01$.

preparation program participants across the nation in 2016 in almost every area. Aspiring Principals resident ratings were notably higher in the areas of Instructional Leadership, Peer Relationships, and Internship Design and Quality across all Aspiring Principals program cohorts. Positive differences in these three survey areas were typically between one-quarter and one-half of the standard deviation in survey-section responses from the 2016 national sample. When comparing New Leaders principals and national results from 2016, differences were positive and statistically significant in the areas of Rigor and Relevance, Faculty Quality, Peer Relationships, and Instructional Leadership.

Perspectives of New Leaders Partner Districts

District goals in partnering with New Leaders typically included increasing the pool of highly qualified leaders, building sustainable principal pipelines from within, developing the capacity to manage principals well, and obtaining assistance with professional development. The interviews with district leaders highlighted the fact that districts had diverse needs, capacities, and priorities, and this diversity was reflected in their goals in partnering with New Leaders. In part, this diversity of needs stemmed from the fact that districts adopted different approaches to, and were at different stages along, the continuum of principal-pipeline development (see Appendix A). One of the interviewed district leaders highlighted the critical role of New Leaders in pipeline-development work, noting that, "Their hand is in the pot as partners." Several other interviewees highlighted the importance of building capacity from within to develop the pipeline. One interviewee noted that New Leaders helped the district build this type of capacity from inside. In interviews conducted after 2016, we found that most districts' goals had changed throughout the course of the partnership.

When talking about New Leaders programming, most interviewees reported appreciating New Leaders' willingness to customize its programs to meet changing district needs. As one interviewee noted, "They do have a quality product, the level of customization helps and is aligned with the mission and goals." While interviewees appreciated New Leaders' customized offerings, one acknowledged increasing competition from other programs: "Our relationship with New Leaders for over ten years speaks volumes. It has been a pillar of support, and they have produced leaders who have transformed schools. But there is now more competition in this sector, and New Leaders needs to keep up with the trend and other partners. There are some others that seem to be gaining traction."

Overall, district leaders agreed that the partnership with New Leaders benefited their district and that the New Leaders principals who had been placed in the last few years had been well prepared and of high quality. One interviewee noted that, over the years, New Leaders principals had become more focused and had served as true change agents in the district, collaborating and sharing their best practices with other schools. District leaders also praised New Leaders principals' instructional leadership skills and use of data. As one interviewee noted, "When I think about those principals who were instructional leaders even before the Common Core requirements, they were New Leaders."

Districts were similarly happy with New Leaders principals' understanding of district needs and New Leaders' responsiveness to issues and concerns raised. Although interviewees told us that the high cost of the programming was the biggest hindrance, respondents mostly agreed that New Leaders provided their district with a good value for the money.

We asked the district leaders to assess 12 statements about New Leaders and its relationship with the districts. They rated their responses to each statement using a five-point scale (where 1 meant they strongly disagreed, 2 that they somewhat disagreed, 3 that they neither agreed nor disagreed, 4 that they somewhat agreed, and 5 that they strongly agreed). In Table 4.7, we show average response scores to each statement in 2017.

Districts cited a smaller overall benefit from their New Leaders partnership in 2017 than in 2014, which could mean that districts improved their internal structures and New Leaders began to play a smaller role in helping solve systemic issues than in the past. For example, a closer look at specific survey results suggested that New Leaders had a smaller influence on how districts selected their principals (due to improved internal capacity), which had been a big benefit and value

Table 4.7
Average Response Scores to Statements in 2017

Statement	Average Rating
a. The partnership with New Leaders has benefited our district/CMO.	3.8
b. New Leaders principals placed in our district in the last few years have been well prepared and of high quality.	4.0
c. New Leaders principals have a positive effect on school climate and teacher effectiveness.	3.5
d. New Leaders understands the needs of our district/CMO.	3.9
e. New Leaders is responsive to issues or concerns raised by our district/ CMO.	4.2
f. New Leaders has influenced how our district/CMO defines effective leadership (i.e., leadership standards).	2.8
g. New Leaders has influenced how our district/CMO selects new principals.	2.4
h. New Leaders has influenced how our district/CMO conducts performance evaluations of sitting principals.	2.6
i. New Leaders has influenced how our district/CMO supervises principals.	2.5
j. New Leaders has influenced how our district/CMO supports the professional development of school leaders (including teacher leaders, aspiring leaders, and/or sitting leaders).	3.2
k. New Leaders is a resource for information about the effective management of principals.	3.0
l. New Leaders provides the district with a good value for the money.	3.8

of New Leaders' involvement in the past. However, the most recent interviews reflected better support for professional development and a better understanding of—and responsiveness to—districts' needs, indicating that New Leaders has become a better partner in regard to specific areas of support. Compared with previous interview responses, more interviewees in 2017 believed that New Leaders was providing a better value for the money.

Summary

This chapter summarized findings from a broad set of analyses that examined intermediate and longer-term outcomes associated with the Aspiring Principals program, as well as perceptions regarding the program's quality. The findings suggest that New Leaders is achieving many of the goals of the Aspiring Principals program. In particular, we found the following:

- The Aspiring Principals program has a high rate of completion.
- Aspiring Principals program participants and district partners view the program favorably.
- Relative to other principal-preparation programs, the Aspiring Principals program has placed a large share of program completers into principal positions.
- Principals who completed the Aspiring Principals program are more likely to stay in their schools for a second year, compared with other principals in the same districts, but they are neither more nor less likely to remain for a third or fourth year.
- Students in K–8 schools led by principals who completed the Aspiring Principals program outperformed students in K–8 schools led by other new principals.

These findings provide useful lessons for anyone who is interested in developing programs to train and support principals, and for researchers who are studying these programs. We discuss these implications in the next chapter.

CHAPTER FIVE

Implications

Our evaluation of New Leaders' Aspiring Principals program relied on a range of methodological approaches to examine the program's effect on districts, schools, and students. Together, our findings suggest implications for researchers and for policymakers and practitioners who are interested in designing, supporting, implementing, and evaluating principal-preparation programs.

New Leaders' Aspiring Principals Program Produces Candidates Who Are Successfully Hired and Retained by Districts

District leaders investing in principal-preparation programs, such as the Aspiring Principals program, or in programs that are considering the adoption of core features of the program seek some assurance that the programs will produce candidates who are able to move directly into the principal role and remain in that position. Our analyses suggest that the Aspiring Principals program successfully placed approximately one-third of its graduates into principal positions between the 2013–2014 and 2017–2018 school years, and it placed an additional one-fifth into assistant principal positions.[1] These placement rates were higher than the five-year placement rates for graduates of the Tennessee

---

[1] Despite a district's investment in the program, the New Leaders partnership does not lead to automatic placement in partner districts. Rather, graduates of the program go through the same hiring and placement process as other qualified candidates.

preparation programs studied by Grissom, Mitani, and Woo (2018), which reported placement rates of between 6 and 17 percent, depending on the program. In addition, the Aspiring Principals program principals were more likely to remain in their positions for a second year than were principals in similar schools in the same districts who were not Aspiring Principals program graduates. Reasons for the higher placement and retention rates of Aspiring Principals graduates were not examined in this study but could reflect both the program's focus on research-based practices that prepare graduates to succeed in school-leadership roles and its emphasis on district partnerships. These findings suggest that districts that choose to partner with New Leaders are likely to reap benefits related to placement and retention, although the differences we observed across districts indicate that contextual factors are likely to play a role in influencing these outcomes.

Students in K–8 Schools Led by New Leaders Principals Outperformed Students in K–8 Schools Led by Other New Principals

Our results suggest that the New Leaders' Aspiring Principals program is preparing principals who are successful at improving student achievement in schools serving K–8 students. In general, our findings suggest that such research-based principal-preparation programs as the Aspiring Principals program are a promising approach to improving school leadership and, as a result, student outcomes. The low number of New Leaders principals placed immediately into high schools precluded us from fully examining the effect of New Leaders principals on these schools.

The Competencies That New Leaders Screened for and Assessed During Residency Are Predictive of Graduates' Later Performance

Principal-preparation programs face a number of practical challenges relating school and student outcomes to program participation. For this reason, it useful to consider whether assessments that are embedded within a preparation program are related to future performance. Our study provides encouraging evidence regarding the potential of such assessments. New Leaders administered a variety of measures to assess residents on competencies it deemed important. Residents' scores on some of these measures predicted their later outcomes as graduates. Specifically, high scores in Human Capital Development, including Instructional Leadership and Adult and Team Leadership, were positively associated with student achievement and attendance, and high scores in Cultural Capital were related to higher principal retention. Principal-preparation programs, states, and districts should consider collecting and using competency data to monitor participants' progress and to tailor further development and support so that candidates can gain the skills and competencies predictive of later effectiveness.

Evaluations of Principal-Preparation Programs Should Examine Multiple Program Features and Outcomes

Evaluations of leadership-preparation programs face special challenges because of small sample sizes, the infeasibility of the experimental design, and difficulty in distinguishing the effect of the program from the effects of other experiences principals have after their programs have ended but before relevant outcomes are realized. By looking at a range of intermediate outcomes at the principal, school, and student levels, our evaluation provides a rich characterization of the ways in which New Leaders principals may influence districts and their schools and students.

Our findings suggest that evaluators should take a broad perspective, consider a range of outcomes, and be open to different views about how different metrics are prioritized or fit together. This approach will ensure that evaluation results speak to a range of stakeholder interests. For example, Grissom, Mitani, and Woo (2018) examined the relationship between programs and a range of outcomes, including completion, licensure examination pass rates, and student outcomes, in Tennessee. The authors found that the ranking of programs differed depending on which outcome was being considered. This is not surprising. A program with a low completion rate and low pass rate on the licensure examination may still produce principal candidates who are successful on the job—if they get the job. Conversely, a program with a high completion rate and a high pass rate on the licensure examination may produce candidates who are, on average, a bit less successful on the job as the program with a low completion and pass rate. But to describe the first program as "highly effective" and the second program as "average" based solely on the school outcomes of program graduates who are hired is misleading. Instead, an evaluation that examines a broad range of outcomes in addition to interim data, such as participants' opinions about the quality of training, can provide information that will meet the needs of various stakeholder groups and allow them to compare programs on the dimensions that are most important to them.

Principal-Preparation Programs Can Help Build Internal Capacity Within Partner Districts

Over the course of this evaluation, we observed a shift in the way district leaders described activities related to the preparation, selection, and support of principals. Several of the district officials we interviewed over the years described New Leaders as a thought partner and enumerated the ways in which New Leaders influenced district leadership standards, hiring, and evaluation. District officials described the prevalence of Aspiring Principals program graduates across the district, not only as principals but as principal supervisors and senior district officials. Such influence is a long-term result of a partnership approach.

Many of the current and former New Leaders partner districts adopted core features of the Aspiring Principals program districtwide. Five districts provided targeted support for new principals for at least a year, in the form of mentoring, coaching, or ongoing professional-development opportunities. Seven districts have a principal candidate pool that is restricted to individuals who demonstrate competencies desired by the district. After partnering with New Leaders, five districts developed their own district-run principal-preparation programs with features similar to the Aspiring Principals program.

These developments suggest that partner districts have been on a journey. To remain a travel partner, New Leaders had to adapt and change. What districts seek from New Leaders will continue to evolve along with the districts' needs and capacity to address those needs internally. To remain relevant, external providers like New Leaders need to adapt and collaborate to provide value for the cost.

District interviewees reported that New Leaders understood the district's needs and was responsive to the feedback they provided about program features and program quality. Our results indicate that this responsiveness has potential payoffs in terms of strong placement rates, retention rates, and school outcomes. Principal preparation requires investments on the part of both aspiring principals and districts. To the extent that those going through a program are hired and retained by the district, both the candidates and the districts win.

Although district partners viewed New Leaders and the principals that came out of its program favorably, several district partners indicated that they were no longer in a partnership with New Leaders, at least with regard to the Aspiring Principals program. In several instances, cost was a driving factor for the termination of the partnership. Other districts continue to partner with New Leaders but have relationships with a number of other partners as well. Kaufman, Gates, et al. (2017) found that residency programs were a key driver of pre-service costs in districts that participated in The Wallace Foundation's Principal Pipeline Initiative. They also found substantial variation in those costs across districts and programs. This suggests that programs partnering with districts should work collaboratively with their partner districts to identify cost-effective strategies for structuring the residency program (something that New Leaders is currently exploring).

Within- and Between-District Analyses Can Provide Complementary Evidence Regarding Program Effectiveness

A program such as New Leaders intentionally partners with districts devoting attention to principal hiring, placement, and support. Such programs also support each district in a way that can ultimately affect practices and outcomes across other schools in the district, even schools that have not hired a principal from that program. Many evaluations of principal-preparation programs rely on within-district comparisons, in large part because district data can support the most-rigorous study designs. Within-district approaches compare the performance of individuals hired by the district and prepared in a particular program with individuals hired by the district but prepared in another program. This comparison approach is useful in ensuring that the two groups of principals receive similar on-the-job supports. But it poses other challenges. If a district has a strong candidate pool, has effective hiring and placement processes, and provides high-quality support to new principals, we would expect that less-qualified candidates would not be hired and that all those who were hired would be effective. In other words, if a district is engaging in effective hiring practices and removing principals who do not perform effectively, the most-relevant outcomes of interest may be the rate at which participants in the program are hired by the district and whether they are retained.

Between-district analysis allows for comparison against principals who are hired by other districts that might not have such robust hiring practices or other supports in place. Comparing school outcomes for new principals in other districts, something we were unable to do in this study, could be a useful approach to understanding the systemic effects of partnering with an organization such as New Leaders, providing evidence that complements the findings from a within-district analysis.

Multiyear Evaluations Are Needed to Capture the Effect of Program Features on School Outcomes

Stakeholders at the state, district, and preparation program levels need to be patient when evaluating the results of a principal preparation program. For a program to affect students, participants must complete the program, be hired as principals, and remain in their positions long enough to have an effect on schools and students. This process can take many years. As a result, it is crucial to approach program evaluation with a long-term perspective and track outcomes over many years.

This is especially true for the high school principalship. Examining the career paths into the high school principalship in North Carolina and Ohio, Burkhauser (2015) found that a vast majority of new high school principals were moving from a principalship in another school or from an assistant principalship. The study suggests that the path from preparation program to high school principalship is more often than not a multistaged one.

Our evaluation of New Leaders focused on individuals who completed the Aspiring Principals program in 2013 or later, and it examined outcomes in their first principalship. Relatively few of these program graduates were initially placed in high schools. That does not mean New Leaders candidates will never move into a principalship at the high school level. A more comprehensive strategy may be needed to examine associations between principals and high school outcomes— one that accounts for a longer pathway into the high school principalship, potentially via a middle school or elementary school principalship or assistant principalship.

The ability to link program participants to downstream outcomes like placement and school outcomes requires statewide data systems that link program participants and district employment. A second-best option is coordination between programs and school districts. This option is a second best because it does not allow programs to track graduates across all potential placements; it also does not allow districts to compare graduates from different preparation programs.

Conclusion

Together, the analyses we conducted to examine intermediate and longer-term outcomes for New Leaders' Aspiring Principals program suggest that the approach that New Leaders has developed to select, train, and support candidates for the principalship is leading to positive outcomes for schools and students. Not only did we find positive relationships between the presence of a New Leaders principal and achievement in K–8 schools, but we also found that the program had a high rate of completion, both participants and district partners expressed favorable views of the program, and rates of retention of New Leaders–trained principals in their schools were relatively high. More research is needed to understand whether a program such as Aspiring Principals could benefit other types of districts or to identify which aspects of the program contribute to its effectiveness. Developers of principal-training programs and leaders of large urban districts that are considering partnering with such programs can look to the New Leaders experience for lessons about ways to improve school leadership development.

Online Appendixes

There are five appendixes available for this report:

- Appendix A, "Profiles of New Leaders Partner Districts"
- Appendix B, "Analysis of School-Level Outcomes"
- Appendix C, "Student Achievement Outcomes Using Student Fixed-Effects Analysis"
- Appendix D, "Analysis of Principal Retention"
- Appendix E, "Analysis of Correlations Between New Leaders' Aspiring Principals Program Competency Metrics and Outcomes."

These appendixes can be downloaded at www.rand.org/t/RR2812.

Bibliography

ABC2 News, "City Schools to Layoff 115 Staff Members by June 30," June 1, 2017. As of September 20, 2017:
http://www.abc2news.com/news/region/baltimore-city/
city-schools-to-lay-off-115-staff-members-by-june-30

Achievement School District, "What We Stand For," undated. As of October 18, 2017:
http://achievementschooldistrict.org/about/

Ahmed-Ullah, N. S., J. Chase, and B. Secter, "CPS Approves Largest School Closure in Chicago's History," *Chicago Tribune*, May 23, 2013. As of October 31, 2017:
http://articles.chicagotribune.com/2013-05-23/news/chi-chicago-school-closings-20130522_1_chicago-teachers-union-byrd-bennett-one-high-school-program

Ahmed-Ullah, N. S., and K. Geiger, "CPS to Lay Off 1,036 Teachers," *Chicago Tribune*, July 19, 2013. As of October 31, 2017:
http://articles.chicagotribune.com/2013-07-1Septembernews/chi-cps-more-layoffs-coming-20130718_1_pension-reform-cps-new-teachers-contract

Alford, A., "A Dozen Years of Change in PGCPS Governance Structure," Prince George's County Advocates for Better Schools, May 18, 2015. As of February 13, 2018:
https://pgcabs.org/2015/05/18/a-dozen-years-of-changes-in-pgcps-governance-structure/

Anthony, L., "Oakland School Board Poised to Make Millions in Cuts," ABC 7 News, November 27, 2017. As of December 1, 2017:
http://abc7news.com/education/
oakland-school-board-poised-to-make-millions-in-cuts/2704271/

Babineau, K., D. Hand, and V. Rossmeier, "The State of Public Education in New Orleans 2016–17," Cowen Institute for Public Education Initiatives, Tulane University, February 2017. As of November 6, 2017:
https://tulane.app.box.com/s/ddngdxbtar9kkn21szyzi6gsplslwqn3

Baker, A., "New York City Teachers Vote for Raise and a Nine-Year Contract," *New York Times*, June 3, 2014. As of November 28, 2017:
https://www.nytimes.com/2014/06/04/nyregion/
new-york-city-teachers-vote-to-approve-9-year-contract.html

Baltimore City Public Schools, "City Schools School Leader Framework and Rubric," undated-a. As of September 20, 2017:
https://www.baltimorecityschools.org/cms/lib/MD01001351/Centricity/
Domain/7994/School%20Leader%20Framework.pdf

———, "Effective School Leaders," undated-b. As of September 20, 2017:
http://www.baltimorecityschools.org/employees/effective_school_leaders

———, "Human Capital Office," undated-c. As of September 20, 2017:
http://www.baltimorecityschools.org/Page/22072

———, "Measuring Effectiveness: The School Leader Effectiveness Evaluation," undated-d. As of September 22, 2017:
http://www.baltimorecityschools.org/Page/21847

———, "School Leadership Opportunities," undated-e. As of September 20, 2017:
http://www.baltimorecityschools.org/site/Default.aspx?PageID=24359

———, "Schools Office," undated-f. As of September 20, 2017:
http://www.baltimorecityschools.org/Page/28480

———, "Application Process for Principal Candidates," last updated May 28, 2010. As of January 25, 2018:
http://www.baltimorecityschools.org/cms/lib/MD01001351/Centricity/
Domain/18/Part_A.pdf

———, "Leadership Development Course Catalogue: SY 14–15," 2014a. As of September 20, 2017:
http://www.baltimorecityschools.org/cms/lib/MD01001351/Centricity/Domain/
7994/Leadership%20Development%20Course%20Catalogue%202014_15.pdf

———, "Growing Great Leaders: School Leadership Development 2014–2015 Overview for Potential Participants," April 2014b. As of September 20, 2017:
http://www.baltimorecityschools.org/cms/lib/MD01001351/Centricity/
Domain/9038/Growing%20Great%20Leaders%20Participant%20Overview%20
April%202014%20%20.pdf

———, *Building a Generation: City Schools' Blueprint for Success*, Baltimore, Md., 2017a. As of September 20, 2017:
http://engage.baltimorecityschools.org/wp-content/uploads/2017/08/
08222017_Blueprint_Booklet_Web.pdf

———, *School Closures and Building Surplusing*, Baltimore, Md., January 13, 2017b. As of September 20, 2017:
http://www.baltimorecityschools.org/cms/lib/MD01001351/Centricity/
Domain/8057/PDF/20170113-FinalClosureSurplusReport.pdf

————, *City Schools Financial Recovery Plan 2017*, Baltimore, Md., August 1, 2017c. As of September 20, 2017:
http://www.boarddocs.com/mabe/bcpss/Board.nsf/files/APTMY758A2A9/$file/Financial%20Recovery%20Plan-%2007.31.17.pdf

————, "District Profile—Spring 2018," 2018. As of June 14, 2018:
http://www.baltimorecityschools.org/cms/lib/MD01001351/Centricity/Domain/8048/999-DistrictProfile.pdf

Benjamini, Y., and Y. Hochberg, "Controlling the False Discovery Rate: A Practical and Powerful Approach to Multiple Testing," *Journal of the Royal Statistical Society, Series B (Methodological)*, Vol. 57, No. 1, 1995, pp. 289–300.

Berlin, J., "Chicago Teacher Strikes: When, How Long and the Reasons Why," *Chicago Tribune*, March 31, 2016. As of October 31, 2017:
http://www.chicagotribune.com/news/local/breaking/ct-chicago-teacher-strikes-timeline-20160331-htmlstory.html

Béteille, T., D. Kalogrides, and S. Loeb, "Stepping Stones: Principal Career Paths and School Outcomes," *Social Science Research*, Vol. 41, No. 4, July 2012, pp. 904–919.

Board of Education of the City of Chicago, "About the Chicago Board of Education," undated. As of October 31, 2017:
http://www.cpsboe.org/about

Board of Education of the City of Chicago and Chicago Public Schools, *Chicago Public Schools Approved Budget 2013–2014*, 2013. As of October 31, 2017:
https://cps.edu/finance/FY14Budget/Documents/FY2014ApprovedBudgetBook.pdf

————, *Chicago Public Schools Proposed Budget 2017–2018*, 2017. As of October 31, 2017:
http://cps.edu/fy18budget/documents/FY18_BudgetBook_amended.pdf

Bowie, L., "Some Critics Call for Thornton's Ouster as Leader of Baltimore Schools," *Baltimore Sun*, February 25, 2016. As of September 13, 2017:
http://www.baltimoresun.com/news/maryland/education/bs-md-thornton-leadership-20160217-story.html

Bradley, B., "CPS CEO Forrest Claypool Announces His Resignation," WGN9 News, December 8, 2017. As of January 15, 2018:
http://wgntv.com/2017/12/08/cps-ceo-forrest-claypool-stepping-down/

Branch, G. F., E. A. Hanushek, and S. G. Rivkin, *Estimating the Effect of Leaders on Public Sector Productivity: The Case of School Principal*, Washington, D.C.: National Bureau of Economic Research, 2012.

Brinson, D., L. Boast, B. Hassel, and N. Kingsland, *New Orleans–Style Education Reform: A Guide for Cities—Lessons Learned, 2004–2010*, New Orleans, La.: New Schools for New Orleans, January 2012. As of November 6, 2017:
http://educatenow.net/wp-content/uploads/2012/02/
New_Orleans_Style_Reform_A_Guide_For_Cities.pdf

Burkhauser, S., *Hello, Goodbye: Three Perspectives on Public School District Staff Turnover*, dissertation, Santa Monica, Calif.: The Frederick S. Pardee RAND Graduate School, RGSD-357, 2015. As of December 11, 2018:
https://www.rand.org/pubs/rgs_dissertations/RGSD357.html

Burkhauser, S., S. M. Gates, L. S. Hamilton, and G. S. Ikemoto, *First-Year Principals in Urban School Districts: How Actions and Working Conditions Relate to Outcomes*, Santa Monica, Calif.: RAND Corporation, TR-1191-NLNS, 2012. As of December 11, 2018:
https://www.rand.org/pubs/technical_reports/TR1191.html

Burnette, D., "Shelby County Closes Three Memphis Schools, Moves Students from Three Others," *Chalkbeat*, March 31, 2015. As of October 18, 2017:
https://tn.chalkbeat.org/posts/tn/2015/03/31/
shelby-county-closes-three-memphis-schools-moves-students-from-three-others/

CBS San Francisco, "Oakland School Board Names New Superintendent," CBS San Francisco and Bay Area, May 22, 2017. As of December 1, 2017:
http://sanfrancisco.cbslocal.com/2017/05/11/
oakland-school-board-new-superintendent-kyla-johnson-trammell/

"Charlotte-Area Charter Schools," *Charlotte Observer*, August 31, 2016. As of October 27, 2017:
http://www.charlotteobserver.com/living/living-here-guide/article99112047.html

Charlotte-Mecklenburg Schools, *Charlotte-Mecklenburg Schools Principal Pipeline Initiative*, undated-a. As of October 20, 2017:
http://edtrust.org/wp-content/uploads/2014/11/A-League-of-Their-Own.pdf

———, *Charlotte-Mecklenburg Schools 2017 Capital Funding Request*, Charlotte, N.C., undated-b. As of October 27, 2017:
http://www.cms.k12.nc.us/mediaroom/Documents/CMS%20Capital%20
Funding%20Needs.pdf

———, "Did You Know?" undated-c. As of October 20, 2017:
http://www.cms.k12.nc.us/mediaroom/aboutus/Pages/Didyouknow.aspx

———, "Enrollment Data," undated-d. As of February 2, 2018:
http://www.cms.k12.nc.us/cmsdepartments/StudentPlacement/PlanningServices/
Pages/Enrollmentdata.aspx

———, "History of CMS," undated-e. As of October 20, 2017:
http://www.cms.k12.nc.us/mediaroom/aboutus/Pages/History.aspx

———, "Principal and Assistant Principal Talent Pools," undated-f. As of October 20, 2017:
http://www.cms.k12.nc.us/Jobs/Pages/
AssistantPrincipalandPrincipalTalentPoolspage.aspx

———, "Principal Pipeline Initiative," undated-g. As of October 20, 2017:
http://www.principalpipeline.com/index.cfm

———, *Strategic Plan 2018: For a Better Tomorrow*, Charlotte, N.C., 2014. As of October 27, 2017:
http://www.cms.k12.nc.us/mediaroom/Documents/
StrategicPlan2018%20rev%20063016.pdf

———, *Fast Facts*, Charlotte, N.C., 2017a. As of October 20, 2017:
http://www.cms.k12.nc.us/mediaroom/Documents/
CMS%202017-2018%20Fast%20Facts.pdf

———, *2017–2018 Proposed Budget Request*, Charlotte, N.C., May 9, 2017b. As of October 20, 2017:
http://www.cms.k12.nc.us/mediaroom/Documents/
Budget%20Book%202017-2018%20Proposed%20Budget%20Request.pdf

Cheney, G. R., and J. Davis, *Gateways to the Principalship: State Power to Improve the Quality of School Leaders*, Washington, D.C.: Center for American Progress, 2011.

Cherone, H., "Here's What Chicago Teachers Won and Lost in Contract Deal," DNA Info News, October 14, 2016. As of October 31, 2017:
https://www.dnainfo.com/chicago/20161014/gladstone-park/
cps-chicago-public-schools-teachers-union-strike

Chicago Principal Partnership, "Meet Our Partners," undated. As of October 31, 2017:
https://chicagoprincipals.org/who-we-are/

Chicago Public Education Fund, "Chicago Principals Fellowship," undated. As of October 31, 2017:
http://thefundchicago.org/our-work/principal-fellowships/
chicago-principals-fellowship/

———, *Chicago's Fight to Keep Top Principals: 2015 School Leadership Report*, Chicago, November 2015. As of November 1, 2017:
http://chicagotonight.wttw.com/sites/default/files/article/file-attachments/
Chicago%27s%20Fight%20to%20Keep%20Top%20Principals.pdf

Chicago Public Schools, *The Next Generation: Chicago's Children, Chicago Public Schools 2013–2018 Action Plan*, Chicago, undated. As of October 31, 2017:
http://cps.edu/pages/actionplan.aspx

———, *CPS Performance Standards for School Leaders Rubric with Critical Attributes*, Chicago, 2015a. As of October 31, 2017:
http://cps.edu/principalevaluation/Documents/PrincipalEvaluationRubric.pdf

———, "Principal Evaluation: Principal Practice," last modified November 25, 2015b. As of October 31, 2017:
http://cps.edu/principalevaluation/Pages/PrincipalPractice.aspx

———, "The Chicago Principal Partnership Launches to Help Ensure Every Public School in Chicago Is Led by a Strong Principal," 2016a. As of November 1, 2017:
http://cps.edu/News/Press_releases/Pages/PR1_11_03_2016.aspx

———, "CPS Leadership," 2016b. As of October 31, 2017:
http://cps.edu/leadership/Pages/leadership.aspx

———, *Principal Eligibility Process Overview and FAQ*, Chicago, 2016c. As of October 31, 2017:
http://cps.edu/PrincipalQuality/Documents/OverviewInstructionsFAQs.pdf

———, *Success Starts Here: Three-Year Vision, 2016–2019*, Chicago, 2016d. As of October 31, 2017:
http://cps.edu/sitecollectiondocuments/cpsvision.pdf

———, "CPS Finalizes District Enrollment for 2017–18 School Year," 2017a. As of January 15, 2018:
http://www.cps.edu/News/Press_releases/Pages/PR1_10_20_2017.aspx

———, "Department of Principal Quality," 2017b. As of October 31, 2017:
http://cps.edu/PrincipalQuality/Pages/PQ.aspx

———, "Department of Principal Quality: Chicago Leadership Collaborative," 2017c. As of October 31, 2017:
http://cps.edu/PrincipalQuality/Pages/Pipeline.aspx

———, "Department of Principal Quality: Independent School Principals (ISP)," 2017d. As of October 30, 2017:
http://cps.edu/PrincipalQuality/Pages/ISP.aspx

———, "Principal Eligibility Assessment Process Application," 2017e. As of October 31, 2017:
http://cps.edu/PrincipalQuality/Pages/Eligibility.aspx

———, "Principalship: Principal Candidates," 2017f. As of October 31, 2017:
http://cps.edu/PrincipalQuality/Pages/Principalship.aspx

Chicago Teachers Union, "Parent, Teacher Protest Today in Push for Classroom Funding, Against Budget Cuts," press release, May 18, 2017. As of October 31, 2017:
https://www.ctunet.com/media/press-releases/
parent-teacher-protest-today-in-push-for-classroom-funding-against-budget-cuts

Coelli, M., and D. A. Green, "Leadership Effects: School Principals and Student Outcomes," *Economics of Education Review*, Vol. 31, No. 1, 2012, pp. 92–109.

Copland, M., and B. Boatright, *Leadership for Transforming High Schools*, Seattle: University of Washington Center for Teaching and Policy, 2006.

Corcoran, A., M. Casserly, R. Price-Baugh, D. Walston, R. Hall, and C. Simon, *Rethinking Leadership: The Changing Role of Principal Supervisors*, Washington, D.C.: Council of Great City Schools, 2013.

Cox, E., "State to Investigate Allegations of Grade Tampering in Prince George's County Schools," *Baltimore Sun*, June 28, 2017. As of February 13, 2018: http://www.baltimoresun.com/news/maryland/education/ bs-md-pg-graduation-rate-investigation-20170628-story.html

Darling-Hammond, L., M. LaPointe, D. Meyerson, and M. T. Orr, *Preparing School Leaders for a Changing World: Lessons from Exemplary Leadership Development Programs*, Stanford, Calif.: Stanford University, 2007.

D.C. Office of the Chief Financial Officer, "2017 GB0 District of Columbia Public Charter School Board," in *FY 2017 Proposed Budget and Financial Plan Congressional Submission*, Washington, D.C., 2016. As of December 18, 2018: https://cfo.dc.gov/node/1148646

Desravines, J., J. Aquino, and B. Fenton, *Breakthrough Principals: A Step-by-Step Guide to Building Stronger Schools*, San Francisco, Calif.: Jossey-Bass, 2016.

District of Columbia Public Charter School Board, *The Performance Management Framework Overview*, Washington, D.C., 2016. As of December 26, 2017: http://www.dcpcsb.org/sites/default/files/The%20Performance%20 Management%20Framework%20Overview%20for%20web%202.12.16.pdf

———, "DC PCSB Staff," 2017a. As of December 27, 2017: http://www.dcpcsb.org/accreditation/dc-pcsb-staff

———, *DC PCSB 2017 Annual Report*, Washington, D.C., 2017b. As of December 26, 2017: http://www.dcpcsb.org/report/pcsb-annual-reports

———, "The Facts," 2017c. As of December 27, 2017: https://data.dcpcsb.org/stories/s/g9zq-zkq5

———, "Job Opportunities," 2017d. As of December 26, 2017: http://www.dcpcsb.org/job-opportunities

———, "Leading a School," 2017e. As of December 26, 2017: http://www.dcpcsb.org/leading-a-school

District of Columbia Public Schools, "The Mary Jane Patterson Fellowship for Aspiring Principals," undated. As of December 15, 2017: https://dcps.dc.gov/page/%0Bmary-jane-patterson-fellowship-aspiring-principals

———, *School Leaders IMPACT: The District of Columbia Public Schools Effectiveness Assessment System for School-Based Personnel*, Washington, D.C., 2016a.

———, *We the People: 2016 Report on DCPS Educators*, Washington, D.C., 2016b. As of December 15, 2017:
https://dcps.dc.gov/page/we-people-2016-report-dcps-educators

———, "A Capital Commitment: 2017–2022," 2017a. As of December 15, 2017:
https://dcps.dc.gov/capitalcommitment

———, "DCPS Fast Facts," 2017b.

———, "DC Public Schools Releases Budget Priorities for Fiscal Year 2018," April 4, 2017c. As of December 15, 2017:
https://dcps.dc.gov/release/
dc-public-schools-releases-budget-priorities-fiscal-year-2018

Dreilinger, D., "New Orleans Has . . . How Many Public Schools This Year?" *Times-Picayune*, October 21, 2015. As of November 6, 2017:
http://www.nola.com/education/index.ssf/2015/10/
new_orleans_school_number.html

———, "New Orleans Has . . . How Many Schools in 2016–17?" *Times-Picayune*, December 14, 2016. As of November 6, 2017:
http://www.nola.com/education/index.ssf/2016/08/
new_orleans_schools_2016-17.html

———, "New Orleans School Lineup: What's Closing, What's Opening This Fall," *Times-Picayune*, August 2, 2017. As of November 6, 2017:
http://www.nola.com/education/index.ssf/2017/08/new_orleans_school_
lineup_2017.html

Dunn, A., "Former CMS Superintendent Heath Morrison Takes Job in Private Sector," *Charlotte Observer*, February 3, 2015. As of October 27, 2017:
http://www.charlotteobserver.com/news/local/education/
article9507674.html#storylink=cpy

"Examiner Local Editorial: Competition, Not Takeover, Is Key to Turnaround at Prince George's County Schools," *Washington Examiner*, March 19, 2013. As of February 13, 2018:
http://www.washingtonexaminer.com/examiner-local-editorial-competition-
not-takeover-is-key-to-turnaround-at-prince-georges-county-schools/
article/2524819

Fuller, E. J., and L. Hollingworth, "Questioning the Use of Outcome Measures to Evaluate Principal Preparation Programs," *Leadership and Policy in Schools*, Vol. 17, No. 2, 2018, pp. 167–188.

Fuller, E. J., L. Hollingworth, and B. An, "The Impact of Personal and Program Characteristics on the Placement of School Leadership Preparation Program Graduates in School Leader Positions," *Educational Administration Quarterly*, Vol. 52, 2016, pp. 643–674.

Gates, S. M., L. S. Hamilton, P. Martorell, S. Burkhauser, P. Heaton, A. Pierson, M. D. Baird, M. Vuollo, J. J. Li, D. C. Lavery, M. Harvey, and K. Gu, *Preparing Principals to Raise Student Achievement: Implementation and Effects of the New Leaders Program in Ten Districts*, Santa Monica, Calif.: RAND Corporation, RR-507-NL, 2014a. As of December 29, 2015:
http://www.rand.org/pubs/research_reports/RR507.html

———, *Preparing Principals to Raise Student Achievement: Implementation and Effects of the New Leaders Program in Ten Districts—Appendix*, Santa Monica, Calif.: RAND Corporation, RR-507/1-NL, 2014b. As of December 29, 2015:
http://www.rand.org/pubs/research_reports/RR507z1.html

Georgetown University, "First-Ever DC Public Schools-Charter Principal Program Launches Through EML Program," 2017. As of December 27, 2017:
https://msb.georgetown.edu/newsroom/news/first-ever-dc-public-schools-charter-principal-program-launches-through-eml-program

George W. Bush Institute, *A Framework for Principal Talent Management*, Dallas, Tex., October 2016.

Goldring, R., and S. Taie, *Principal Attrition and Mobility: Results from the 2012– 13 Principal Follow-Up Survey*, Washington, D.C.: National Center for Education Statistics, 2014.

"Graphic: Timeline of Chicago Public Schools CEOs," *Chicago Tribune*, 2015. As of October 31, 2017:
http://www.chicagotribune.com/chi-cps-ceo-history-timeline-gfx-20150602-photogallery.html

Green, E. L., "Baltimore Schools' CEO to Be Replaced by Former Academics Chief," *Baltimore Sun*, May 3, 2016. As of September 8, 2017:
http://www.baltimoresun.com/news/maryland/education/bs-md-thornton-out-20160503-story.html

Grissom, J. A., and B. Bartanen, "Principal Effectiveness and Principal Turnover," *Education Finance and Policy*, advance online publication, 2018. As of November 30, 2018:
https://www.mitpressjournals.org/doi/abs/10.1162/edfp_a_00256

Grissom, J. A., R. S. Blissett, and H. Mitani, "Evaluating School Principals: Supervisor Ratings of Principal Practice and Principal Job Performance," *Educational Evaluation and Policy Analysis*, Vol. 40, No. 3, 2018, pp. 446–472.

Grissom, J. A., D. Kalogrides, and S. Loeb, "Using Student Test Scores to Measure Principal Performance," *Educational Evaluation and Policy Analysis*, Vol. 37, 2015, pp. 3–28.

Grissom, J. A., and S. Loeb, "Triangulating Principal Effectiveness: How the Perspectives of Parents, Teachers and Assistant Principals Identify the Central Importance of Managerial Skills," *American Educational Research Journal*, Vol. 48, No. 5, 2011, pp. 1091–1123.

Grissom, J. A., S. Loeb, and B. Master, "Effective Instructional Time Use for School Leaders: Longitudinal Evidence from Observations of Principals," *Educational Researcher*, Vol. 42, No. 8, 2013, pp. 433–444.

Grissom, J. A., H. Mitani, and D. S. Woo, "Principal Preparation Programs and Principal Outcomes," *Educational Administration Quarterly*, advance online publication, 2018, pp. 1–43.

Harris, E. A., and M. Fernandez, "Is Richard Carranza Ready to Run America's Biggest School System?" *New York Times*, March 18, 2018. As of June 13, 2018: https://www.nytimes.com/2018/03/18/nyregion/carranza-new-york-schools-chancellor.html?action=click&module=RelatedCoverage&pgtype=Article&region=Footer

Helms, A. D., "More Meck Families Choose Charters, but CMS Still Dominates the School Choice Market," *Charlotte Observer*, February 22, 2017. As of October 27, 2017: http://www.charlotteobserver.com/news/local/education/article134232234.html

Hensley, S. B., "DC Public Schools Chancellor Announces Departure," *Washington's Top News*, June 29, 2016. As of December 15, 2017: https://wtop.com/dc/2016/06/dc-public-schools-chancellor-announces-departure/

Herman, Rebecca Epstein, Susan M. Gates, Aziza Arifkhanova, Andriy Bega, Emilio Chavez-Herrerias, Eugeniu Han, Mark Harris, Jennifer Tamargo, and Stephani Wrabel, *School Leadership Interventions Under the Every Student Succeeds Act: Evidence Review—Updated and Expanded*, Santa Monica, Calif.: RAND Corporation, RR-1550-3-WF, 2017. As of August 10, 2018: http://www.rand.org/pubs/research_reports/RR1550-3.html

Hutchins, D. J., J. L. Epstein, and S. B. Sheldon, *How Do Principals' Reports of Leadership Practices Reflect UEF Categories, Levers, and Concepts?* Baltimore, Md.: Johns Hopkins University, 2012.

Illinois Department of Public Health, *2006 Illinois Resident Births by County and Plurality*, Springfield, 2007. As of January 15, 2018: http://www.dph.illinois.gov/sites/default/files/publications/2006-multiple-il-resident-births.pdf

———, *Live Births by Resident County and Plurality, Illinois Residents, 2015*, Springfield, 2016. As of January 15, 2018: http://dph.illinois.gov/sites/default/files/publications/Multiple-Births-by-County-2015.pdf

Illinois Network of Charter Schools, "Charter Enrollment Growth," 2015. As of January 15, 2018:
https://www.incschools.org/tableau/?post=32&type=enrollment_facts&index=2-1

Kaufman, Julia H., Susan M. Gates, Melody Harvey, Yanlin Wang, and Mark Barrett, *What It Takes to Operate and Maintain Principal Pipelines: Costs and Other Resources*, Santa Monica, Calif.: RAND Corporation, RR-2078-WF, 2017. As of June 13, 2018:
http://www.rand.org/pubs/research_reports/RR2078.html

Kebede, L. F., "Hopson Wants to Invest in Memphis Teacher Raises, Student Supports, Struggling Schools," *Chalkbeat*, March 13, 2017. As of October 18, 2017:
https://www.chalkbeat.org/posts/tn/2017/03/13/hopson-wants-to-invest-in-memphis-teacher-raises-student-supports-struggling-schools/

Larsen, E., M. Clifford, M. Lemke, D. Chambers, and A. Swanlund, *Following the Leaders: An Analysis of Graduate Effectiveness from Five Principal Preparation Programs*, Dallas, Tex.: George W. Bush Institute, 2016a.

———, *Developing Leaders: The Importance—and the Challenges—of Evaluating Principal Preparation Programs*, Dallas, Tex.: George W. Bush Institute, 2016b.

Leithwood, K., K. S. Louis, S. Anderson, and K. Wahlstrom, *How Leadership Influences Student Learning: A Review of the Evidence Linking Leadership to Student Learning*, New York: The Wallace Foundation, 2004.

Levin, S., "Oakland Teachers Reach Tentative Contract Agreement with Salary Increases, Seniority Rights," *East Bay Express*, May 14, 2015. As of December 1, 2017:
https://www.eastbayexpress.com/SevenDays/archives/2015/05/14/oakland-teachers-reach-tentative-contract-agreement-with-salary-increases-seniority-rights

Louisiana Department of Education, *Bulletin 125—Standards for Educational Leaders in Louisiana*, Louisiana Administrative Code, March 2011. As of November 8, 2017:
https://www.teachlouisiana.net/Prospect.aspx?PageID=501

———, *Louisiana Leader Performance Evaluation Rubric*, 2014. As of November 8, 2017:
https://www.louisianabelieves.com/docs/default-source/key-compass-resources/2014-2015-compass-leader-rubric.pdf?sfvrsn=14

———, *Annual Financial Report 2015–16*, 2016. As of November 8, 2017:
http://www.louisianabelieves.com/resources/library/financial-data

———, "Compass New Evaluator Training 2017–2018," 2017a. As of November 8, 2017:
http://www.louisianabelieves.com/docs/default-source/key-compass-resources/2017-2018-compass-new-evaluator-training.pdf?sfvrsn=4

————, "Compass Updates 2017–2018 Implementation," 2017b. As of November 8, 2017:
http://www.louisianabelieves.com/docs/default-source/key-compass-resources/2017-2018-district-compass-updates.pdf?sfvrsn=4

————, "News Release: Recovery School District Aligns Organization and Leadership with Statewide Strategy," March 16, 2017c. As of November 8, 2017:
https://www.louisianabelieves.com/newsroom/news-releases/2017/03/16/recovery-school-district-aligns-organization-and-leadership-with-statewide-strategy

Marimow, A. E., "D.C. Public School Teachers Approve New Contract," *Washington Post*, September 9, 2017. As of December 15, 2017:
https://www.washingtonpost.com/local/education/dc-public-school-teachers-approve-new-contract/2017/09/09/6d22c6ae-958b-11e7-8754-d478688d23b4_story.html?utm_term=.ff86460dd098

Maryland Department of Health, *Maryland Vital Statistics Annual Report 2016*, 2016. As of June 12, 2018:
https://health.maryland.gov/vsa/Documents/2016_AnnualReport.WebVersion.pdf

Marzano, R., T. Waters, and B. McNulty, *School Leadership That Works: From Research to Results*, Alexandria, Va.: ASCD, 2005.

Masterson, M., "CPS Looks to Recruit, Retain Quality Principals Through New Partnership," WTTW Chicago, November 3, 2016. As of November 1, 2017:
http://chicagotonight.wttw.com/2016/11/03/cps-looks-recruit-retain-quality-principals-through-new-partnership

Matos, A., "Antwan Wilson Confirmed as Chancellor of DC Public Schools," *Washington Post*, December 20, 2016. As of December 15, 2017:
https://www.washingtonpost.com/local/education/antwan-wilson-confirmed-as-chancellor-of-dc-public-schools/2016/12/20/be7a4aa4-c6ce-11e6-bf4b-2c064d32a4bf_story.html?utm_term=.75693c85db5b

————, "For the First Time, a DC Charter School Has Voted to Create a Teachers Union," *Washington Post*, June 16, 2017. As of December 26, 2017:
https://www.washingtonpost.com/local/education/for-the-first-time-a-dc-charter-school-has-voted-to-create-a-teachers-union/2017/06/16/935f1a1e-52bc-11e7-b064-828ba60fbb98_story.html?utm_term=.3b4a738f5723

"Memphis City Schools Superintendent Kriner Cash Resigns," *Memphis Business Journal*, January 11, 2013. As of February 15, 2018:
https://www.bizjournals.com/memphis/blog/morning_call/2013/01/memphis-city-schools-superintendent.html

Miller, A., "Principal Turnover and Student Achievement," *Economics of Education Review*, Vol. 36, No. C, 2013, pp. 60–72.

Monroe, K., "Oakland USD 2016–17 First Interim Report Letter," Alameda County Office of Education, January 17, 2017. As of December 1, 2017:
https://drive.google.com/file/d/0BxMqlDlfSN03UURIcFJsbUlzNjg/view

New Leaders, "Leadership Practice Improvement (LPI)," undated-a.

———, "Our Mission," undated-b. As of December 10, 2018:
http://www.newleaders.org/about/

———, *New Leaders Urban Excellence Framework*, New York, 2011.

———, *Transformational Leadership Framework*, New York, 2016.

———, *Selection Standards*, New York, 2017. As of December 18, 2018:
https://newleaders.org/wp-content/uploads/2018/02/FY18SelectionStandards.pdf

New York City Charter School Center, "Charter School Enrollment and Trends,"
2017a. As of November 28, 2017:
http://www.nyccharterschools.org/sites/default/files/resources/
Charter-Enrollment-Trends.pdf

———, "NYC Charter School Facts 2017–2018," 2017b. As of November 28,
2017:
http://www.nyccharterschools.org/sites/default/files/resources/
NYC-Charter-Facts.pdf

New York City Department of Education, "Mayor Elect De Blasio Appoints
Carmen Fariña as Schools Chancellor," December 30, 2013a. As of January 4,
2019:
https://www.schools.nyc.gov/about-us/news/
announcements/contentdetails/2013/12/30/
mayor-elect-de-blasio-appoints-carmen-fariña-as-schools-chancellor

———, *2013–14 Quality Review Rubric*, 2013b.

———, *Strong Schools, Strong Communities: A New Approach to Supporting New
York City's Public Schools and All of Our Students*, New York, 2015. As of January 7,
2019:
http://proxy.nycboe.org/NR/rdonlyres/C955EF12-EBBC-4B41-AF8D-
20597C55DF0C/0/StrongSchoolsStrongCommunities_NYCDOE.pdf

———, "About Us," 2017a.

———, *Field Guide for the 2017–18 Principal Performance Review: A Guide for
Principals and Evaluators*, New York, 2017b.

———, "Initiatives for Strong Schools, Strong Communities," 2017c.

———, "Principal Candidate Pool," 2017d.

———, *2017–18 Charter School Directory*, New York, 2017e. As of November 28,
2017:
https://newyorkcitydepartmentofeducati.app.box.com/s/
aymaralizkov11uwbzikmrz2xk9qu2j6

Ni, Y., L. Hollingworth, A. Rorrer, and D. Pounder, "The Evaluation of Educational Leadership Preparation Programs," in M. D. Young and G. M. Crow, eds., *The Handbook of Research on the Education of School Leaders*, 2nd ed., New York: Routledge, 2017, pp. 285–307.

Oakland Unified School District, "School Leadership Recruitment," 2012.

———, *Fast Facts 2013–14*, Oakland, Calif., 2013. As of December 1, 2017:
https://drive.google.com/drive/u/0/folders/0B6QEqRqzjxxzOGllWlBUS2d2ZXc

———, *Fast Facts 2014–15*, Oakland, Calif., 2014. As of December 1, 2017:
https://drive.google.com/drive/u/0/folders/0B6QEqRqzjxxzOGllWlBUS2d2ZXc

———, *Fast Facts 2015–16*, Oakland, Calif., 2015a. As of December 1, 2017:
https://drive.google.com/drive/u/0/folders/0B6QEqRqzjxxzOGllWlBUS2d2ZXc

———, *Pathway to Excellence: 2015–2020 Strategic Plan*, Oakland, Calif., 2015b. As of December 1, 2017:
https://www.ousd.org/domain/3

———, *2015–16 OUSD Leadership Growth and Development System Handbook*, Oakland, Calif., 2015c. As of December 1, 2017:
https://docs.google.com/viewerng/viewer?url=https://www.ousd.org//cms/lib/CA01001176/Centricity/Domain/3423/2015-16+LGDS+Handbook.pdf

———, *Fast Facts 2016–17*, Oakland, Calif., 2016. As of December 1, 2017:
https://drive.google.com/drive/u/0/folders/0B6QEqRqzjxxzOGllWlBUS2d2ZXc

———, "Budget Prioritization 2017–18," 2017a. As of December 1, 2017:
https://www.ousd.org/Page/15885

———, *Fast Facts 2017–18*, Oakland, Calif., 2017b. As of August 27, 2018:
https://drive.google.com/file/d2018vKVTDbTxKOTlnQGSZmITyiuNI-1Am_R/view

———, "Leadership Growth and Development System Overview," 2017c. As of December 1, 2017:
https://www.ousd.org/domain/3423

Oakland Unified School District and United Administrators of Oakland Schools, "Agreement Between Oakland Unified School District and United Administrators of Oakland Schools (UAOS) for the Period July 1, 2014–June 30, 2017," 2014. As of December 1, 2017:
https://ousd.legistar.com/LegislationDetail.aspx?ID=3089769&GUID=838C5501-A7DD-4F72-AA73-0DF4C7F7752E&Options=ID|Text|&Search=UAOS

Orleans Parish School Board, "2018 General Fund Budget," June 15, 2017. As of November 8, 2017:
http://opsb.us/wp-content/uploads/2012/10/170524_Budget-Book_v35.pdf

Orr, M. T., and S. Orphanos, "How Graduate-Level Preparation Influences the Effectiveness of School Leaders: A Comparison of the Outcomes of Exemplary and Conventional Leadership Preparation Programs for Principals," *Educational Administration Quarterly*, Vol. 47, 2011, pp. 18–70.

Perez, J., "Chicago Teachers Union: No Confidence Vote in CPS Chief Also Aimed at Mayor," *Chicago Tribune*, May 24, 2017. As of October 31, 2017: http://www.chicagotribune.com/news/local/breaking/ct-karen-lewis-chicago-teachers-confidence-vote-met-20170523-story.html

Perez, J., and D. Dardick, "CPS Proposes $5.7 Billion Budget, Including $269 Million in Help from City," *Chicago Tribune*, August 11, 2017. As of October 31, 2017:
http://www.chicagotribune.com/news/local/politics/ct-chicago-public-schools-city-funding-met-0812-20170811-story.html

Pounder, D. G., and R. Merrill, "Job Desirability of the High School Principalship: A Job Choice Theory Perspective," *Educational Administration Quarterly*, Vol. 37. No. 2, 2001, pp. 25–57.

Pounder, D., Y. Ni, K. Winn, S. Korach, A. Rorrer, and M. D. Young, *Findings from the 2016 Inspire-Graduate (G) Survey*, Charlottesville, Va.: University Council for Educational Administration, 2016.

Prince George's County Public Schools, *2013 PGCPS Bridge to Excellence Master Plan Annual Update*, Upper Marlboro, Md., 2013. As of December 8, 2017: http://www.pgcps.org/masterplan/

———, *2014 PGCPS Bridge to Excellence Master Plan Annual Update*, Upper Marlboro, Md., 2014a. As of December 8, 2017: http://www.pgcps.org/masterplan/

———, *Administrative Procedure 4113: Principal Selection Process*, Upper Marlboro, Md., 2014b. As of December 8, 2017: https://drive.google.com/file/d/0BzaqNq4behBDWm5TT3NxXzVtTkE/edit

———, *2015 PGCPS Bridge to Excellence Master Plan Annual Update*, Upper Marlboro, Md., 2015. As of December 8, 2017: http://www.pgcps.org/masterplan/

———, *2016 PGCPS Bridge to Excellence Master Plan Annual Update*, Upper Marlboro, Md., 2016a. As of December 8, 2017: http://www.pgcps.org/masterplan/

———, "Principal Evaluation," Office of Employee Performance and Evaluation, 2016b. As of December 7, 2017: http://www.pgcps.org/employeeperformanceandevaluation/index.aspx?id=220914

———, *2017 PGCPS Bridge to Excellence Master Plan Annual Update*, Upper Marlboro, Md., 2017a. As of December 8, 2017: http://www.pgcps.org/masterplan/

————, "Chief Executive Officer," 2017b. As of December 8, 2017:
http://www.pgcps.org/ceo/

————, "List of All Schools by School Type," 2017c. As of December 8, 2017:
http://www.pgcps.org/list-of-schools-by-type/

Prothero, A., "All New Orleans Schools Set to Return to Local Oversight,"
Education Week, May 12, 2016. As of November 7, 2017:
https://www.edweek.org/ew/articles/2016/05/12/
all-new-orleans-schools-set-to-return.html

Rangel, V. S., "A Review of the Literature on Principal Turnover," *Review of Educational Research*, Vol. 88, No. 1, 2018, pp. 87–124.

Reardon, S., and R. Hinze-Pifer, *Test Score Growth Among Chicago Public School Students, 2009–2014*, Stanford, Calif.: Center for Education Policy Analysis, 2017.

Recovery School District, *2014 Annual Report*, Shreveport, La., 2015. As of November 6, 2017:
http://lrsd.entest.org/2015%20RSD%20Annual%20Report.pdf

————, *2015 Annual Report*, Shreveport, La., 2016. As of November 6, 2017:
http://lrsd.entest.org/2015%20RSD%20Annual%20Report.pdf

————, *2016 Annual Report*, Shreveport, La., 2017. As of November 6, 2017:
http://lrsd.entest.org/
RSD%202016%20annual%20report%20updated%203_27_17.pdf

Rojas, R., "Dennis Walcott, Former Schools Chancellor, Is Named CEO of Queens Library," *New York Times*, March 1, 2016. As of November 28, 2017:
https://www.nytimes.com/2016/03/02/nyregion/
dennis-walcott-former-schools-chancellor-is-named-ceo-of-queens-library.html

Santelises, S. B., T. Jones, and A. Alvarez, "Public Charter Schools Policy: Compliance Report Review of SY 2015–16," presentation to the Baltimore City Board of School Commissioners, May 23, 2017. As of September 20, 2017:
http://www.baltimorecityschools.org/cms/lib/MD01001351/Centricity/
Domain/8783/2017_IHB_Charter_Policy_Compliance_SY15-16.pdf

School Leaders Network, *Churn: The High Cost of Principal Turnover*, Hinsdale, Mass., 2014.

Shelby County Board of Education, *Destination 2025: Shelby Schools Annual Report*, Columbiana, Ala., 2015a. As of October 18, 2017:
http://www.scsk12.org/2025/

————, *Effective School Leadership Policy*, Columbiana, Ala., 2015b. As of October, 27, 2017:
http://www.scsk12.org/policy/files/files/4000%20Personnel/
4050%20Effective%20School%20Leadership.pdf

Shelby County Schools, *Destination 2025: Annual Report 2016*, Columbiana, Ala., 2016. As of October 18, 2017:
http://www.scsk12.org/2025/

———, *District Budget: Fiscal Year 2017–2018*, Columbiana, Ala., 2017. As of October 18, 2017:
http://www.scsk12.org/finance/files/2016/
FY17 DISTRICT BUDGET_FINAL 101416.pdf

———, "Shelby County Schools by the Numbers," 2018. As of August 15, 2018:
http://www.scsk12.org/

ShelbyPLUS, "Shelby Plus Is No Longer Active," undated. As of February 16, 2018:
http://shelbyplus.org/welcome

Smith, N., *The Louisiana Recovery School District: Lessons for the Buckeye State*, Thomas B. Washington, D.C., Fordham Institute, 2012. As of November 6, 2017:
http://files.eric.ed.gov/fulltext/ED528943.pdf

Stein, P., "DC Schools Budget Emphasizes Alternative High Schools and Programs," *Washington Post*, February 16, 2016. As of December 15, 2017:
https://www.washingtonpost.com/local/education/dc-schools-budget-emphasizes-alternative-high-schools-and-programs/2016/02/16/8fccfdac-d4d3-11e5-9823-02b905009f99_story.html?utm_term=.8da8d5a59515

Stein, P., and E. Brown, "DC Schools Chancellor Kaya Henderson to Step Down, Leaving Legacy of Progress," *Washington Post*, June 29, 2016. As of December 15, 2017:
https://www.washingtonpost.com/local/education/dc-schools-chancellor-kaya-henderson-to-step-down-leaving-legacy-of-progress/2016/06/29/1189e7e6-3df8-11e6-80bc-d06711fd2125_story.html?utm_term=.4bdff2cd1804

Tafolla, M., "Opinion: Strong Leadership Needed to Fix Oakland School Finances," *Mercury News*, November 14, 2017. As of December 1, 2017:
http://www.mercurynews.com/2017/11/14/opinion-strong-leadership-needed-to-fix-oakland-school-finances/

Tennessee Educator Acceleration Model, "Administrator Evaluation," 2017. As of October 18, 2017:
http://team-tn.org/evaluation/administrator-evaluation/

Tennessee State Board of Education, *Learning Centered Leadership Policy: Appendix C Tennessee Instructional Leadership Standards*, 2015. As of October 18, 2017:
http://team-tn.org/wp-content/uploads/2013/08/TILS_5.101.pdf

Tobias, S. P., and J. Shorman, "A Wichita High School with 12 Assistant Principals? Kobach's Claim Is Not True" *Wichita Eagle*, September 12, 2018. As of December 4, 2018:
https://www.kansas.com/news/local/education/article218190440.html#storylink=cpy

Toth, S., "Maxwell Welcomed 'Home' as Prince George's Schools' CEO," *Baltimore Sun*, June 28, 2013. As of December 7, 2017:
http://www.baltimoresun.com/news/maryland/howard/laurel/
ph-ll-maxwell-superintendent-0704-20130704-story.html

Tucker, J., "Oakland Schools Chief Antwan Wilson Takes Job in Washington, DC," *SF Gate*, November 22, 2016. As of December 15, 2017:
http://www.sfgate.com/bayarea/article/
Oakland-schools-superintendent-takes-new-job-in-10630171.php

Turnbull, B. J., L. M. Anderson, D. L. Riley, J. R. MacFarlane, and D. K. Aladjem, *The Principal Pipeline Initiative in Action*, Vol. 5 of *Building a Stronger Principalship*, Washington, D.C.: Policy Studies Associates, 2016. As of November 28, 2017:
https://eric.ed.gov/?id=ED570472

Turnbull, B. J., D. L. Riley, E. R. Arcaira, L. M. Anderson, and J. R. MacFarlane, *Six Districts Begin the Principal Pipeline Initiative*, Vol. 1 of *Building a Stronger Principalship*, Washington, D.C.: Policy Studies Associates, July 2013.

WGN and D. Rebik, "CPS Lays Off More Than 950 Staff, Including 356 Teachers; New Budget Delayed," *WGN News*, August 7, 2017. As of October 31, 2017:
http://wgntv.com/2017/08/07/cps-lays-off-950-including-356-teachers/

What Works Clearinghouse, *Procedures Handbook, Version 4.0*, October 2017. As of November 30, 2018:
https://ies.ed.gov/ncee/wwc/Docs/referenceresources/
wwc_procedures_handbook_v4.pdf

Wiggins, O., "Charter Schools Grow in Prince George's County," *Washington Post*, February 21, 2012. As of December 8, 2017:
https://www.washingtonpost.com/local/education/
charter-schools-grow-in-prince-georges-county/2012/02/15/
gIQADtaCRR_story.html?utm_term=.9cfd98be8c3b

Winn, K., D. Pounder, C. Groth, S. Korach, A. Rorrer, and M. D. Young, *Findings from the 2017 Inspire Leaders in Practice (LP) Survey*, Charlottesville, Va.: University Council for Educational Administration, 2018.

WWC—*See* What Works Clearinghouse.